FLAVORS of HAV

Recipes Celebrating Hawaii's Diversity

**Tested recipes from members and friends of the
Child & Family Service Guild**

FLAVORS *of* HAWAII

Recipes That Celebrate Hawaii's Diversity

The Child & Family Service (CFS) Guild is a group of dedicated volunteers whose purpose is to support the work of CFS through fundraisers and special events. All proceeds from this cookbook will benefit Child & Family Service programs.

Hawaii's people have depended on Child & Family Service since 1899. Today CFS is Hawaii's most comprehensive, private non-profit human service organization with programs on Oahu, Kauai, Maui, Lanai, Molokai and the Big Island. Sensitive to Hawaii's cultural diversity, the professional staff at CFS provides services to families and individuals regardless of sex, ethnic background, age or the ability to pay. Child & Family Service offers quality programs for children, teens, families, adults, employees and the elderly.

This cookbook is a compilation of favorite recipes,
not necessarily original ones.

For information on ordering additional copies, call or write:

Child & Family Service Guild
200 N. Vineyard Blvd., Bldg. B
Honolulu, HI 96817
Phone: (808) 543-8441 • Fax (808) 524-8383
Honolulu, HI 96817

Order blanks for additional copies of **Flavors of Hawaii**
are available at the back of this book.

ISBN 0966450108

Library of Congress catalog card number 98-86091

Copyright © 1998
All rights reserved

First printing 10,000 copies
October, 1998

Printed in the USA by

WIMMER

The Wimmer Companies

Memphis

1-800-548-2537

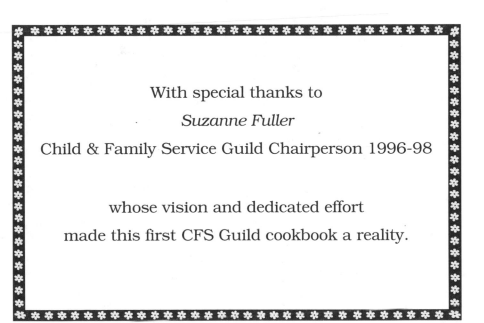

With special thanks to

Suzanne Fuller

Child & Family Service Guild Chairperson 1996-98

whose vision and dedicated effort

made this first CFS Guild cookbook a reality.

About the artist...

AL FURTADO

Alfred Furtado captures vivid memories of the people of the islands of Hawaii, from the exciting and colorful dancers to the beautiful children and ethnic cultures.

He has been a working artist, teacher and lecturer for more than 40 years. His fine artwork has been acknowledged through private showings and sales to hotels and other commercial institutions, as well as to private collectors everywhere.

For those who live here, the paintings bring forth memories of family. For those who were island born and moved away, they evoke nostalgia. For visitors to the islands fortunate enough to have met local people and enjoyed being part of the culture, the art is a remembrance of a unique experience.

Mr. Furtado's work is being shown in several of Hawaii's leading galleries. His art is also available on limited edition prints and published on cards by Island Heritage.

• *1629 Wilder Ave., #501* • *Honolulu, Hawaii, 96822* • *phone: (808) 941-9545* • *(e-mail) leialfurt@aol.com*

Celebrating One Hundred Years of Service

The year is 1899, the cusp of a new century and a time when Honolulu was approaching 60,000 in population. People were just getting used to the idea that they were now a part of the United States of America. There was a near breathless anticipation of a building and financial boom that would transform the very soul of the downtown and the community.

Critical human service needs also existed in 1899 and, in response, caring island residents founded Associated Charities and dedicated it to helping those in need. Today, that organization, now known as Child & Family Service, is Hawaii's most comprehensive, private, non-profit human service agency.

Flavors of Hawaii is a collection of favorite recipes, tested and assembled by the Child & Family Service Guild and friends. This first CFS Guild cookbook is a celebration of both the first hundred years of CFS and the rich cultural diversity that is Hawaii. The recipes are as diverse as the people of Hawaii.

Since its founding in 1899, Child & Family Service has worked hard to keep pace with and anticipate the burgeoning needs of Hawaii's families and, today, has more than 30 programs and services statewide. The CFS Guild is a group of quietly-committed and dedicated volunteers who work throughout the year to assist Child & Family Service in its efforts to improve the quality of life for families in Hawaii. Proceeds from the sale of **Flavors of Hawaii** will support programs that target early-childhood health and development needs, teach parenting skills, provide counseling and protective shelter for victims of violence and abuse, and offer employee assistance and elder care services.

Child & Family Service and the CFS Guild thank you for your purchase of **Flavors of Hawaii**. May the enjoyment you find in sampling its selection of recipes be matched by the satisfaction you take in knowing that you have helped Child & Family Service help Hawaii.

Historic Background

By the time the first Polynesian spotted the dim lip of distant Mauna Kea at the sea's edge, those who had survived mankind's maiden voyage to the islands of Hawaii must have thought the waves would never end. We can only imagine the courage it took to sustain them and the joy that accompanied their celebration of thanksgiving upon landing. It would be wonderful to know what that first meal was. It was probably made up of the remnants of taro, coconut, banana, breadfruit and sweet potatoes that they managed to save during their voyage.

The tradition of Hawaiian cooking began more than a thousand years ago with the arrival of those first Polynesians. They brought with them in their canoes plants and seeds of taro, coconuts, bananas, breadfruit and sweet potatoes as well as chickens, dogs, pigs and dried fish. Inevitably, eating became a social function, frequently connected with religious ceremonies and regulated by rules and laws. Taro was their main staple. They pounded the cooked roots into a paste called "poi." Poi is still eaten today and is available in local markets.

Hawaiians caught fish in the ocean or in walled-in sea ponds. The small fish were eaten raw, bones and all. Larger fish were wrapped in ti leaves and cooked over a fire or together with other foods in an "imu," an earth-pit oven. On special occasions, a traditional feast called a "luau" was held for large groups of people. Women gathered the food, men did the preparation and cooking. The feast lasted many hours. Music, chants and hula dancers entertained the guests. Traditional luaus for special events, such as birthdays, are still popular today. Tourist versions are presented for hotel guests.

In 1778, Captain Cook rediscovered the Islands and changed the lives of the Hawaiians forever. Not long thereafter, ships arrived from Europe and New England. An economy based first on whaling and trading, then sugar and pineapple, brought new people with their own traditions in food. Missionaries, who depended largely on food staples sent to them from their homeland and gifts from visiting sea captains, introduced breads, pies and other sweet desserts, molasses, sugar, cheese, butter, oil, salt and other spices. They would often trade their imported foods for fresh local fruits and vegetables.

The sugar plantations needed manual labor, and by the mid-1840s the first wave of Chinese immigrants from the Canton region arrived, and with them chickens, ducks, and seeds of fruits and vegetables, including mustard cabbage, water chestnuts, lychee, soy beans, peanuts, rice, coffee and mandarin oranges. Later, Japanese immigrants came as plantation workers, replacing the Chinese, many of whom had opened stores to supply the plantation workers with their needs. The Japanese cultivated soy beans, daikon, eggplant and cabbage. They boiled, fried or steamed their food and seasoned it with soy sauce.

Korean plantation workers arrived at the turn of the century and brought with them pickled cabbage (kim chee) and marinated beef with spicy seasonings. Kim chee is very popular among locals today and is available in island markets.

The first Europeans to arrive in the Islands between 1878 and 1887 were Portuguese, most of them from the Madeira Islands and the Azores. Although they quickly adopted foods from other ethnic groups, they had their own methods of food preparation. Portuguese bean soup, malasadas and sweet bread are still popular today.

Filipinos, most of them from Ilocanos, the northwestern part of the Island of Luzon, arrived between 1907 and 1915. They brought a cooking style influenced by the Spanish (using tomatoes and garlic), Chinese (wrapping filling in lumpia wrappers), and Malaysian traders (cooking with coconut milk). The multi-cultural influences continued as more Europeans and Mainlanders arrived and contributed additional foods. In more recent times, the gastronomical melting pot continued to expand with arrivals from Thailand, Cambodia, Vietnam and other countries.

As people from different cultures learned to appreciate the diversity of food, recipes changed. Many dishes were adapted to what was available in the islands. The flavors of Hawaii can be found in those adaptations in Hawaiian homes and restaurants today. Welcome to a rainbow of culinary delights.

Child & Family Service Guild
Flavors of Hawaii Committee

Editor-in-chief: Suzanne Fuller

Committee Members

Daisy Asher

Sandi Chun

Hannelore Herbig

Lorraine Lunow-Luke

Jill MacMillan

Bobbe Nunes

Ginger Plasch

Anne Rautio

Sandy Rogin

Cheryl Suzuki

Linda Tam

Rhonda Thomas

Bonny Tinebra

Marian Turney

Kimi Uto

Lynda Yonamine

Sandi Yorong

Table of Contents

- *Check the Glossary for definitions of and substitutions for various foods.*
- *Unless noted otherwise, all nutritional information is based on per serving amounts according to yield of recipe.*

A warm mahalo from the CFS Guild to

Hilton Hawaiian Village

Aloha Airlines

GE Capital Hawaii, Inc.

Pupus (Appetizers)

Roquefort and Pesto Cheese Loaf

A delightful mix of mild and pungent flavors.

1 8-ounce package cream cheese, softened

1 3.5-ounce package Roquefort cheese, at room temperature

1 cup loosely packed spinach, rinsed and thoroughly dried

¾ cup loosely packed fresh Italian parsley

¼ cup loosely packed fresh basil leaves

1 teaspoon minced garlic

½ cup olive oil

¼ cup finely chopped walnuts

1 cup freshly grated Parmesan cheese

¼ cup sun-dried tomatoes, patted dry, minced

2 tablespoons minced Kalamata olives

whole fresh basil leaves for garnish

crackers or toasted baguette slices

- Line small loaf pan with plastic wrap, leaving edges hanging over pan sides.

- Combine cream cheese and Roquefort until smooth. Set aside.

- In food processor, combine spinach, parsley, basil and garlic. Slowly drizzle oil through feed tube while processor is running. Blend pesto until smooth. Transfer to mixing bowl and add walnuts and Parmesan cheese. Stir thoroughly.

- Spread one third of cheese mixture evenly over bottom of prepared pan. Next spread half of pesto mixture. Sprinkle half of tomatoes and half of olives on top. Repeat three layers. Finish with remaining third of cheese mixture.

- Cover with ends of plastic wrap liner.

- Refrigerate 24 hours.

- Before serving, allow loaf to come to room temperature, about 30 minutes. Invert onto serving plate. Garnish top with basil leaves.

- Serve with crackers or toasted baguette slices.

Yields 10-12 servings.

Marinated Shrimp

1 clove garlic
1 cup extra virgin olive oil
⅔ cup rice vinegar
  juice of 1 lemon
2 teaspoons dried oregano
½ teaspoon red pepper
  flakes
1 teaspoon salt
2 pounds medium shrimp,
  cooked, shelled and
  deveined
1 Maui onion, thinly sliced
1 green bell pepper, thinly
  sliced
1 red bell pepper, thinly
  sliced

- Mash garlic with flat side of knife and place in olive oil for 1 to 6 hours. Discard garlic.
- Combine vinegar, lemon juice, oregano, red pepper flakes and salt. Mix well. Whisk in olive oil.
- Toss together shrimp, onion, and red and green peppers in sauce.
- Refrigerate 2 hours prior to serving.

Yields 12 -15 servings.

Variation: Serve over salad greens as an entrée.

Spinach Balls

2 10-ounce packages frozen,
  chopped spinach
1 6-ounce box chicken
  stuffing mix
1 cup grated Parmesan
  cheese
6 eggs, slightly beaten
¾ cup melted butter
1-2 teaspoons Tabasco sauce,
  optional

- Preheat oven to 350°.
- Thaw, drain and squeeze dry chopped spinach.
- Mix all ingredients together until well combined. Form mixture into half-dollar size balls. Place on cookie sheet.
- Bake 20 minutes. Serve at room temperature.

Yields 24 servings.

Maui Onion Spread

3 large Maui onions, finely
   chopped
1 cup sugar
½ cup white wine vinegar
1 cup water
½ cup mayonnaise
½ teaspoon celery seed
   assorted crackers

- Place chopped onions in glass bowl.
- In saucepan, mix sugar, vinegar and water. Bring to boil. Remove from heat and cool. Pour over onions. Cover bowl.
- Refrigerate at least 12 hours.
- Drain onions well. Mix with mayonnaise and celery seed.
- Refrigerate at least 2 hours.
- Serve with crackers.

Yields 8 servings.

Teriyaki Sirloin Kabob

2 pounds sirloin steak
½ cup soy sauce
3 tablespoons sugar
1 tablespoon red wine
   vinegar
½ teaspoon minced fresh
   ginger or ⅛ teaspoon
   ground ginger
1 clove garlic, minced

- Slice steak on diagonal into 2x1x¼-inch strips.
- Combine soy sauce, sugar, vinegar, ginger and garlic. Pour over meat. Marinate 30 minutes.
- Preheat broiler or start grill.
- Thread steak on skewers.
- Barbecue or broil to desired doneness.

Yields 36 servings.

40 calories; 2 grams fat; 36% percent calories from fat; 64 mg. sodium

Meat Sticks with Peanut Sauce

2 pounds boneless meat
  (chicken, pork or beef),
  cut into bite-size pieces
Marinade
Peanut Sauce
crispy fried onions

Marinade

2 shallots, sliced
1 clove garlic, crushed
2 tablespoons soy sauce
  pinch hot chili pepper
1 teaspoon ground
  coriander
1 teaspoon ground ginger
1 tablespoon vinegar
1 tablespoon peanut (or
  vegetable) oil

- Combine all marinade ingredients. Pour over meat. Marinate 2 hours or overnight. Before grilling, prepare peanut sauce.

Peanut Sauce

1 tablespoon peanut oil
2 shallots, sliced
  chili pepper and salt
  to taste
1 clove garlic, crushed
1½ cups water
½ cup chunky peanut butter
1 tablespoon lemon juice
1 teaspoon brown sugar (or
  soy sauce)

- Heat oil. Sauté shallots, chili pepper, salt and garlic until shallots are soft. Quickly add water. After water boils, add peanut butter, lemon juice and sugar (or soy sauce). Stir well.

- Continue boiling and stirring until sauce is thickened, about 3 minutes.

- Preheat grill. Thread meat on skewers.

- Grill 5-8 minutes or until done. Pour sauce over grilled meat. Sprinkle with crispy fried onions.

Yields 8-10 servings.

Pesto Torte

A good "make-ahead" party dish.

3 cups fresh basil leaves
1 cup fresh parsley leaves
¾ cup freshly grated Parmesan cheese
3 tablespoons pine nuts or macadamia nuts
2 tablespoons olive oil
11 ounces cream cheese
½ cup butter
½ teaspoon lemon juice
½ teaspoon Tabasco sauce
whole basil leaves for garnish
pita bread, crackers or lavosh

- In food processor, combine basil, parsley, Parmesan cheese and nuts. Whirl until finely chopped. Slowly add olive oil while machine is running. Blend until well combined. Transfer to bowl.

- In clean food-processor bowl, combine cream cheese, butter, lemon juice and Tabasco. Blend until smooth.

- Line 3-cup mold with cheese cloth. Place half of cheese mixture as first layer. Smooth basil mixture over top. Cover with remaining cheese mixture.

- Refrigerate 3 hours.

- Unmold. Garnish with whole basil leaves. Serve with pita bread, crackers or lavosh.

Yields 12 servings.

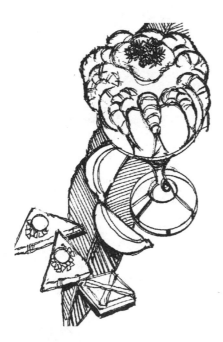

Marinated Olives

1½ pounds (drained weight) assorted Greek or Sicilian olives
1-2 sprigs fresh thyme
1-2 sprigs fresh sage
1-2 sprigs fresh rosemary
1-2 sprigs fresh oregano
2 bay leaves
3 cloves garlic, sliced
olive oil
balsamic vinegar

- Combine olives, herbs and garlic in glass or stainless steel bowl. Cover halfway with mixture of 3 parts olive oil to 1 part vinegar. Cover.
- Refrigerate overnight, turning one or two times.
- When serving, use slotted utensil and spoon from bottom to bring up olives fully submerged in marinade.

Yields 3 cups.

Note: Olives keep indefinitely in refrigerator. Stir them, now and then, to keep moist. Also, olive marinade can be used in salad dressings.

Tomato and Maui Onion Salsa

4 small tomatoes, chopped
1 small Maui onion, finely chopped
1 cup coarsely chopped fresh cilantro leaves
½ teaspoon cumin
½ fresh jalapeño pepper, minced
juice of ½ lime or ¼ lemon, or to taste
freshly ground pepper
1 clove garlic, minced
1 small avocado, diced
salt, to taste

- Combine all ingredients. Refrigerate 1 hour to allow flavors to blend.

Yields 12 (¼ cup) servings.

27 calories; 2 grams fat; 47% calories from fat; 5 mg. sodium

Raw Tako (Octopus)

3 pounds island tako (octopus)
⅛ cup sesame oil
4 tablespoons ko choo jang sauce (Korean chili pepper/garlic paste)
1 cup chopped green onion
5 tablespoons soy sauce
1 tablespoon inamona (crushed kukui nut paste)
2 small Hawaiian chili peppers, finely chopped
Hawaiian salt, to taste

- Skin octopus and cut into bite-size pieces.

- In large mixing bowl, thoroughly mix octopus, sesame oil and ko choo jang sauce. Stir in green onion, soy sauce, inamona, and chili peppers. Add Hawaiian salt to taste.

- Refrigerate 4 hours.

Yields 20 servings.

Easy Smoked Ahi Dip

2 cups smoked ahi (tuna), papio (travally), salmon, nairigi (marlin) or other smoked fish
1 tablespoon roasted garlic
1 cup sour cream or softened cream cheese
freshly grated black pepper
2 tablespoons finely sliced chives
chips or cut vegetables for dipping

- Flake smoked fish.

- Squeeze roasted garlic from husk. Mash and mix with sour cream or cream cheese. Stir in smoked fish and pepper to taste. Place in serving dish.

- Cover and chill at least 1 hour or as long as 2 days ahead to blend flavors. Before serving, garnish with chives.

- Serve with chips or freshly cut vegetables.

Yields 3 cups.

Kiwi Kabobs with Apricot Dip

Kabobs

4 **medium kiwis**

2 **large navel oranges or blood oranges**

2 **bananas**

2 **tablespoons fresh lemon juice mixed with 2 tablespoons water**

16 **bite-size fresh pineapple chunks or fresh strawberries**

Apricot Dip

Apricot Dipping Sauce

¾ **cup mashed, canned apricots**

¼ **teaspoon grated orange peel**

2 **tablespoons honey**

¼ **teaspoon each cinnamon and nutmeg (or ⅜ teaspoon curry powder)**

1¼ **cups low-fat vanilla yogurt**

1 **cup low-fat cream cheese**

- Peel kiwis and cut into quarters lengthwise. Peel oranges and cut into 4 thick crosswise slices. Remove seeds and cut each slice in half. Peel bananas. Cut each into 8 chunks. Dip kiwis and bananas into lemon water to prevent discoloration.

- Thread one section of each fruit on skewer. Serve with sauce for dipping. Or serve fruit in bowl with sauce on side.

- Combine apricots, orange peel, honey and spices.

- In separate bowl, mix or process yogurt and cream cheese until smooth. Add to fruit mixture and stir until combined. Cover and chill until ready to serve.

Yields 16 fruit kabobs, 2¼ cups dip.

Pineapple-Marlin Kabobs

⅓ cup light soy sauce

1 tablespoon fresh orange juice

2 tablespoons chopped green onion

1 tablespoon vegetable or extra-virgin olive oil

1 tablespoon grated fresh ginger root

1 tablespoon toasted sesame seeds

1 teaspoon honey

¼ teaspoon freshly ground black pepper

1½ pounds marlin or other firm-fleshed fish, cut into 1¼-inch chunks

12 bite-size fresh pineapple pieces

- Blend soy sauce, orange juice, green onion, oil, ginger root, sesame seeds, honey and pepper until smooth. Pour over fish. Marinate for 1 hour.

- Preheat broiler or grill.

- Thread fish chunks on skewers, alternating with pineapple pieces.

- If broiling, broil 5 minutes, turn, brush with marinade, and broil 3 more minutes.

- If grilling, cook 3 minutes, turn, brush with marinade and cook 2 more minutes. Be careful not to overcook or fish will harden.

Yields 8-12 servings.

Note: Serve with rice, baked sweet potatoes and steamed snow peas for dinner for four.

Tortellini and Shrimp

1½ pounds medium shrimp, cooked and peeled
½ cup diced celery
1 pound cheese-filled tortellini, cooked and drained
  Marinade

- Combine shrimp, celery, tortellini and marinade in large bowl. Toss gently. Chill 24 hours.

Marinade

⅓ cup olive oil
2 tablespoons red wine vinegar
¼ cup ketchup
2 teaspoons Dijon mustard
1 tablespoon lemon juice
1 tablespoon horseradish
2 cloves garlic, minced
1 teaspoon hot pepper sauce
½ teaspoon salt
½ teaspoon black pepper

- Whisk all ingredients until well blended.

Yields 15-20 servings.

Variation: For light entrée serving six to eight, spoon onto bed of romaine lettuce and garnish with fresh lemon wedges.

Aloha Clams

2 10-ounce packages frozen spinach, chopped
2 6.5-ounce cans minced clams
2 eggs, beaten
1¼ cups bread crumbs
⅓ cup Parmesan cheese
⅓ cup Romano cheese
¼ cup minced onion
  salt and pepper, to taste
  wonton skins
  oil for frying

- Thaw spinach. Squeeze out excess water.

- Drain clams and save juice.

- Mix spinach and clams with eggs, bread crumbs, cheeses, minced onion, salt and pepper.

- Place small teaspoonful of mixture in center of wonton skin. Moisten edges with clam juice and fold.

- Heat oil for frying. Deep fry until golden.

Yields 12-16 servings.

Orange Muffin Bites

1 cup sugar
½ cup unsalted butter
2 eggs
1 teaspoon baking soda
1 cup buttermilk
2 cups sifted flour
½ teaspoon salt
1 cup raisins
   zest of 1 orange
   juice of 1 orange
½ pound smoked turkey
   breast
¾ cup mango chutney or
   pineapple salsa

- Preheat oven to 400°. Grease small muffin tins for 30 muffins.

- In mixer bowl, cream sugar and butter. Add eggs and beat until fluffy.

- Add baking soda to buttermilk. Sift together flour and salt.

- Add buttermilk alternately with flour mixture to creamed butter. Stir until combined.

- Grind raisins and orange zest in food processor. Add to batter and mix. Spoon batter into prepared muffin tins. Bake 12 minutes until golden brown and firm to touch.

- Brush freshly baked muffins with orange juice. Cool 5 minutes in pan. Cool muffins completely before cutting in half.

- Place small slice of turkey on bottom half of each muffin. Add about ½ teaspoon chutney or salsa and cover with top of muffin. Serve.

Yields 30 servings.

Variation: Try these other combinations: roast beef with horseradish, ham with mustard, turkey with cranberry relish and duck breast with plum jam.

127 calories; 4 grams fat; 25% calories from fat; 201 mg. sodium

Heated Oysters with Hollandaise Sauce

6 oysters
12 spinach leaves
  butter
  salt and pepper
  homemade or packaged
    Hollandaise Sauce

- Preheat broiler.

- Open oysters and reserve juice and meat. Clean and dry bottom shells.

- Sauté 1-2 leaves of spinach per oyster in a small amount of butter. Season with salt and pepper to taste.

- Slightly heat oysters in oyster juice but do not cook.

- Prepare Hollandaise Sauce.

- Place spinach in shell and top with oyster. Cover with Hollandaise Sauce. Place under broiler just to color.

Yields 2 servings.

Artichoke Nibbles

The combined cheese and artichoke flavors make this pupu special.

2 6.5-ounce jars marinated artichoke hearts, drained and chopped (reserve marinade from 1 jar of artichoke hearts)
1 small onion, finely minced
1 clove garlic, finely minced
4 eggs
¼ cup fine bread crumbs
¼ teaspoon salt
⅛ teaspoon pepper
⅛ teaspoon oregano
⅛ teaspoon Tabasco sauce
2 cups shredded sharp cheddar cheese
2 tablespoons minced fresh parsley

- Preheat oven to 325°. Grease 7x11x2-inch baking pan.

- Heat reserved marinade in frying pan. Add artichoke hearts, onion and garlic. Sauté until onion is limp.

- In bowl, beat eggs. Add bread crumbs, salt, pepper, oregano and Tabasco. Stir in cheese, parsley and artichoke-onion mixture. Pour into prepared pan.

- Bake 30 minutes until set. Let cool in pan. Cut into 1-inch squares.

- Serve warm.

Yields 16 servings.

Papaya and Kiwi Salsa with Brie

An elegant pupu for a dinner party.

Papaya and Kiwi Salsa

3 cups peeled, diced ripe papaya
¾ cup peeled, diced kiwi
2 tablespoons chopped green or red bell pepper
1½ tablespoons chopped shallot
2 tablespoons chopped fresh cilantro
1½ tablespoons fresh lime juice
⅛ teaspoon ground allspice

- Combine papaya, kiwi, pepper, shallot, cilantro, lime juice and allspice in bowl. Mix well. Set aside.

Tortillas and Brie

8 flour tortillas, each cut into 8 wedges
4 ounces Brie cheese
papaya and kiwi salsa

- Preheat oven to 350°.
- Place tortilla wedges on baking sheet.
- Bake 10 minutes or until crisp. Set aside.
- Place cheese on ovenproof serving dish.
- Bake 10 minutes or until heated through.
- Surround cheese with prepared tortilla wedges. Serve salsa on side.

Yields 16 servings.

Vietnamese Spring Rolls

10 dried shiitake mushrooms
and/or dried black
fungus (fragrant
mushroom that adds
crunchiness, usually
available in dried form)
1 large onion, chopped
½ pound jicama, or one
6-ounce can water
chestnuts, chopped
1 2-ounce package rice
sticks
½ pound ground pork
½ pound ground chicken
2 teaspoons freshly ground
black pepper
1 tablespoon Thai fish sauce,
or 1 teaspoon salt
½ teaspoon sugar
1 package frozen lumpia
wrappers
oil for deep frying
Manoa lettuce
fresh mint leaves
Dipping Sauce

- Soak dried mushrooms and black fungus in warm water. Wash, rinse and cut out stem and hard parts. Pat dry. Mince.
- Squeeze moisture out of jicama and onion. The drier the ingredients, the better. Rolls will not fry crisply when wet.
- Soak rice sticks until soft; drain and cut into small pieces.
- Combine mushrooms, black fungus, onion, jicama and rice sticks with pork, chicken, pepper, fish sauce and sugar. Mix well.
- Thaw lumpia wrappers. Separate each sheet carefully. Put 1 tablespoon of filling at edge, fold each side and roll up. Set aside on paper towel until ready to deep fry.
- Heat oil to 300° over medium heat. Deep fry spring rolls about 10-12 minutes until filling is thoroughly cooked and lightly browned.
- Serve hot spring rolls on lettuce leaf with mint and Dipping Sauce.

Dipping Sauce

½ cup Thai fish sauce
1½ cups water
2 tablespoons sugar, or
more to taste
1 tablespoon vinegar
Carrot and Daikon Relish

- Boil fish sauce with water and sugar about 5 minutes until sugar dissolves. Add vinegar. Let cool. Add relish, drained, before serving.

(Continued)

(Vietnamese Spring Rolls, continued)

Carrot and Daikon Relish

1 **carrot, shredded**
1 **medium daikon, shredded**
½ **cup water**
1 **teaspoon vinegar**
1 **tablespoon sugar**
  pinch salt

- Mix carrot and daikon with water, vinegar, sugar and salt. Refrigerate until ready to serve. Remove carrots and daikon from liquid, and add to Dipping Sauce before serving.

Yields 26-28 servings.

Salmon and Pesto Mold

7 **ounces cooked salmon**
  filet or one 7½-ounce
  can red salmon, drained,
  flaked (skin and bones
  removed)
12 **ounces cream cheese,**
  softened, divided
2 **teaspoons chopped fresh**
  dill
¼ **cup pesto**
1 **tablespoon butter,**
  softened
2 **tablespoons finely**
  chopped green onion or
  chives
¼ **teaspoon freshly ground**
  pepper
  dill sprig for garnish
  crackers or baguette
  slices

- Line bottom and sides of three-cup mold or loaf pan with plastic wrap.
- Combine salmon, 4 ounces cream cheese and dill. Mix well. Spread evenly over bottom of prepared pan.
- Chill 10 minutes.
- Spread pesto over salmon mixture.
- Combine 8 ounces cream cheese, butter, green onion and pepper. Mix well. Drop by spoonfuls over pesto and gently spread. Cover and chill at least 6 hours.
- Invert pan onto serving platter and remove plastic wrap. Let stand 15 minutes at room temperature. Garnish with fresh dill sprigs. Serve with crackers or baguette slices.

Yields 8-12 servings.

Goi Cuon (Vietnamese Summer Rolls)

Sauce

3-4 **cloves garlic, chopped**
  1 **teaspoon oil**
  1 **10-ounce jar hoisin sauce**
  1 **cup chicken broth**
  1 **tablespoon peanut butter**
  1 **teaspoon sugar**

- Sauté garlic in oil. Add hoisin sauce, chicken broth, peanut butter and sugar. Bring to boil. Set aside.

Carrot and Daikon Relish

  1 **teaspoon vinegar**
  1 **tablespoon sugar**
  ½ **cup water**
    pinch salt
  1 **carrot, shredded**
  1 **daikon, shredded**

- Mix all ingredients. Chill.

Summer Rolls

  ½ **pound pork butt**
  ½ **pound medium shrimp**
  1 **egg**
    rice noodles
    Manoa lettuce
    mint leaves
    chives
  1 **package large rice paper**
    roasted peanuts, chopped

Boil pork 20 minutes or until fully cooked.

- Boil shrimp; cool, peel and devein. Split in half and set aside.

- Prepare egg as omelet.

- Slice pork, shrimp and egg each into 20 thin strips.

- Boil rice noodles and rinse. Set aside.

- Wash and dry lettuce, mint and chives. Set aside.

- Quickly dip rice paper into large shallow bowl partially filled with lukewarm water. Lift out, shake off moisture and place on absorbent towel. Turn once on towel. Always use both hands to handle rice paper.

(Continued)

(Goi Cuon [Vietnamese Summer Rolls], continued)

- Place rice paper on cutting board. Place flat piece of lettuce at edge of rice paper. On top, add small amounts of pork, mint and rice noodle. Roll 2 times. Fold in end flaps and roll once. (While rolling, press to make tight and hold in filling.)

- Place 2 halves of shrimp, red side down, on rice paper. Roll. Add 1 strip egg. Roll.

- Place few sprigs of chives on rice paper and finish rolling. Serve within an hour. Cover so rice paper does not dry out. Damp rice paper cannot be refrigerated without becoming chewy.

- Place sauce in individual bowls for serving. Add some drained Carrot and Daikon Relish. Sprinkle with roasted peanuts. Dip rolls into sauce and enjoy.

Yields about 20 rolls.

Ginger Dip

¼ **cup finely chopped Maui onion**

1 **8-ounce can water chestnuts, drained, finely chopped**

2 **teaspoons crystallized ginger, minced**

1 **cup mayonnaise**

1 **cup sour cream**

¼ **cup chopped fresh cilantro**

1 **tablespoon soy sauce**
  dash Tabasco sauce
  corn chips or raw vegetables

- Combine all ingredients. Mix well. Make 1-2 days ahead to allow flavors to blend.

- Serve with corn chips or raw vegetables.

Yields 2½-3 cups.

Scampi

½ cup butter
½ cup olive oil
1 tablespoon lemon juice
¼ cup chopped green onion
1 tablespoon finely chopped
    garlic
1 teaspoon salt
    freshly ground pepper
2½ pounds large shrimp,
    peeled, deveined, washed
    and dried
15 slices high-quality bread
4 tablespoons finely
    chopped parsley

- Preheat broiler to highest temperature.

- Melt butter and oil over low heat. Add lemon juice, onion and garlic. Stir slowly and cook until flavors blend. Add salt and pepper to taste.

- Place shrimp on broiler pan. Pour sauce over shrimp.

- Broil 3-4 inches from heat 4 minutes. Turn shrimp over and broil until pink, about 4 minutes. Do not overcook.

- While shrimp is broiling, toast bread slices and cut each into 4 triangles.

- Remove shrimp from broiler pan and dip toast into liquid left in pan.

- Place toast on warmed plate, top with shrimp and sprinkle with parsley.

Yields 8-10 servings.

Quesadillas

2 cups shredded Colby and
   Monterey Jack cheeses
6 7- or 8-inch flour tortillas
3 tablespoons canned,
   diced, green chili
   peppers, drained
3 tablespoons chopped
   green onion, including
   tops
   salsa

- Preheat oven to 300°.
- Sprinkle ⅓ cup cheese over half of each tortilla. Top with chili peppers and green onion. Fold tortillas in half; press gently.
- In 10-inch skillet, cook 2 quesadillas at a time over medium heat for 2-3 minutes or until lightly brown. Turn once. Remove from pan, place on baking sheet and keep warm in oven. Repeat with remaining quesadillas.
- To serve, cut into wedges. Serve with salsa.

Yields 6 servings.

Tortilla Wedges

12 7- or 8-inch flour tortillas

- Preheat oven to 350°.
- Cut each tortilla into 8 wedges. Place single layer of wedges in large baking pan.
- Bake 5-10 minutes until dry and crisp. Repeat until all wedges are baked. Cool.
- Place in tightly closed container. Store at room temperature up to 4 days or in freezer up to 3 weeks.

Yields 84-96 wedges.

Shrimp and Cucumber Slices

Shrimp and Cucumbers

36 medium shrimp in their shells
crab boil seasoning
2-3 cucumbers, peeled and sliced
Garlic Mayonnaise
dill sprigs for garnish

- Cook shrimp, in their shells, in boiling water seasoned with crab boil seasoning. Peel and chill.

- Spread each cucumber slice with 1 teaspoon of Garlic Mayonnaise. Top with 1 shrimp. Chill until serving time. Garnish with dill sprig. Best if made one hour before serving.

Garlic Mayonnaise

1 egg
1½ tablespoons lemon juice
1½ tablespoons white wine vinegar
1 teaspoon salt
3 cloves garlic, minced
½ cup olive oil
½ cup vegetable oil
⅓ cup chopped, unsalted macadamia nuts

- Place egg, lemon juice, vinegar, salt and garlic in blender. Process until blended. With motor running, slowly pour in olive and vegetable oils. Add nuts and blend a few seconds more. Cover and chill.

Yields 36 pieces.

Variation: Leftover pupus can be chopped and mixed with cooked, chilled pasta to make a refreshing salad.

40 calories; 4 grams fat; 79% calories from fat; 42 mg. sodium

Crostini with Dried Tomato and Feta Spread

1 3.5-ounce jar oil-packed dried tomatoes, drained (reserve oil)
1 baguette
¼ cup finely chopped onion
1 teaspoon capers, drained, or 1 tablespoon chopped, pitted ripe olives
2 cloves garlic, minced
1 teaspoon minced basil
1 3-ounce package cream cheese, softened
2 tablespoons milk
1 cup feta or soft goat cheese, crumbled (about 4 ounces)

- Preheat oven to 400°.
- Cut baguette on the bias into ¼-inch slices. Lightly brush one side of each slice with reserved oil from tomato jar. Place on baking sheet.
- Bake 4 minutes. Turn slices over and bake another 4 minutes.
- Finely chop tomatoes. Mix with onion, capers, garlic and basil. Set aside.
- Beat cream cheese and milk with electric mixer until smooth. Stir in feta cheese and blend until smooth.
- Spread cheese mixture on oiled side of toasted bread slices. Top with small amount of tomato mixture. Serve immediately.

Yields 40 servings.

Easy Kaki Mochi (Seasoned Rice Crackers)

¼ cup butter
¼ cup light corn syrup
¼ cup vegetable oil
¼ cup sugar
1 tablespoon soy sauce
1 12.3-ounce package bite-size corn and wheat cereal squares
1 1.05-ounce package furikake nori (seasoned seaweed)

- Preheat oven to 250°.
- In small saucepan, melt butter. Add syrup, oil, sugar, and soy sauce. Stir until sugar dissolves.
- Put cereal into large baking pan. Pour syrup over cereal and mix well. Stir in furikake.
- Bake 45 minutes, stirring every 15 minutes. Cool. Store in airtight container.

Yields 3 quarts.

Beijing Chicken Wings with Orange Marinade

½ cup soy sauce
¼ cup dry sherry
⅓ cup hoisin sauce
6 green onions, finely chopped
2 cloves garlic, minced
¼ cup cider vinegar
½ cup honey
1 teaspoon finely grated fresh orange zest
1 teaspoon finely grated fresh lemon zest
1 teaspoon Tabasco sauce, or to taste
4 pounds chicken wings, tips cut off and wings separated at joint

- In large bowl, stir together soy sauce, sherry, hoisin sauce, green onions, garlic, vinegar, honey, orange and lemon zest and Tabasco. Reserve ½ cup marinade and refrigerate. Pour marinade over chicken wings, stirring to coat them well.

- Cover and marinate in refrigerator, stirring occasionally, for 4 hours or overnight.

- Preheat oven to 375°.

- Drain chicken. Discard marinade. Transfer chicken to rack on foil-lined broiler pan.

- Bake on middle oven rack, turning and basting with reserved marinade every 20 minutes up to 1 hour, until nicely browned.

Yields 12-16 servings.

Island Cheese Spread

2 8-ounce packages cream cheese, softened
1 tablespoon seasoned salt
2 cups chopped macadamia nuts, divided
½ cup chopped green bell pepper
¼ cup finely chopped Maui onion
1 8-ounce can crushed pineapple, well drained
crackers or toasted baguettes

- Combine cream cheese, seasoned salt, 1 cup nuts, pepper, onion and pineapple.

- Form into log shape and roll in remaining 1 cup nuts. Wrap and chill.

- Serve with crackers or sliced baguettes.

Yields 10-12 servings.

Brandied Brie with Grapes

1 **4-inch wheel Brie cheese**
1 **teaspoon brandy**
1 **teaspoon sugar**
½ **cup coarsely chopped, seedless red grapes; reserve 3 grapes for garnish**
1½ **teaspoons chopped fresh basil; reserve small sprig of basil for garnish**
2 **tablespoons chopped, roasted, salted, macadamia nuts**
crackers

- Cut cheese in half horizontally.
- Combine brandy and sugar. Brush cut surfaces of cheese with mixture.
- Combine grapes and basil. Spread on bottom half. Top with nuts. Replace top half of cheese over mixture. Cover and refrigerate.
- One half hour prior to baking, take cheese out of refrigerator and let stand at room temperature.
- Preheat oven to 350°. Lightly oil pie plate or shallow baking dish.
- Place Brie in plate or dish.
- Bake 10-15 minutes.
- Place on serving plate. Slice 3 grapes in half. Arrange grape halves and sprig of basil decoratively on top of Brie. Serve with crackers.

Yields 8-10 servings.

Hot Crabmeat Appetizer

1 8-ounce package cream cheese, softened

1½ cups crabmeat (one 7.5-ounce can), picked over to remove bits of shell

2 tablespoons finely chopped onion

2 tablespoons milk

½ tablespoon horseradish, creamy style

¼ teaspoon salt, or to taste freshly ground pepper, to taste

⅓ cup sliced almonds, toasted

toasted baguette or crackers

- Preheat oven to 375°.
- Combine cream cheese, crabmeat, onion, milk, horseradish, salt and pepper. Mix until blended.
- Spoon into 9-inch pie plate or dish. Sprinkle with almonds.
- Bake 15 minutes.
- Serve with sliced baguette or crackers.

Yields 8-10 servings.

Salmon Loaf Classic - Revisited

½ pound grilled salmon

1 8-ounce package cream cheese, softened

1 tablespoon lemon juice

2 teaspoons grated onion

1 teaspoon prepared horseradish

1 teaspoon salt

3 tablespoons chopped parsley

½ cup chopped pecans

crackers or toasted baguettes

lemon wedges, chopped red onion, capers and freshly ground pepper, to garnish

- Skin, debone and flake salmon. Combine salmon, cream cheese, lemon juice, onion, horseradish and salt. Mix well. Chill several hours or overnight.
- Mold into a loaf.
- Mix together parsley and pecans. Roll salmon loaf in parsley and pecan mixture.
- Serve with crackers or toasted baguettes. Sprinkle with lemon, onion, capers and freshly ground pepper, if desired.

Yields 12-15 servings.

Variation: Substitute 1 16-ounce can red salmon and ¼ teaspoon liquid smoke for grilled salmon.

Japanese Tiny Chicken Drumsticks

2-3 pounds chicken
    drumettes
    flour
    vegetable oil for frying
½ cup soy sauce
6 tablespoons sugar
1-2 cloves garlic, chopped
    dash of Tabasco sauce
2 green onions, chopped
1 ounce sesame seeds,
    lightly toasted

- Roll drumettes in flour and deep fry. Blot carefully with paper towels.

- Combine soy sauce, sugar, garlic, Tabasco and green onions. Dip drumettes into sauce and roll in sesame seeds.

Yields 8-16 servings.

Hummus

A delicious Middle Eastern, chickpea-tahini spread filled with spices, richness and protein.

1 15.5-ounce can garbanzo
    beans (chickpeas),
    drained
3 medium cloves garlic, or
    to taste, minced
1½ teaspoons salt
    juice of 2 medium lemons,
    extra lemon juice as
    needed
¼ cup tahini (sesame paste)
¼ cup finely minced green
    onions
2 tablespoons olive oil,
    additional olive oil as
    needed
    freshly ground black
    pepper
    dash of cayenne
    toasted wedges of pita
    bread or raw vegetable
    sticks

- Combine beans, garlic, salt, juice of 2 lemons, tahini, green onions and 2 tablespoons olive oil in food processor. Process until smooth.

- Taste. Add more olive oil and/or lemon juice, if needed.

- Mound in bowl. Smooth top. Drizzle with olive oil and lemon juice.

- Serve with pita or vegetable sticks as dip.

Yields 8-16 servings.

Variation: Serve as sandwich filling with lettuce, tomato, minced green onion, shredded carrot and feta cheese in pocket of pita bread.

Potstickers

Potstickers

1½ cups cooked, shredded chicken breast

7 ounces firm tofu

3 tablespoons fresh basil, finely minced

1-2 shiitake mushrooms, cooked, stem removed and finely chopped (4 tablespoons)

¼ cup black olives, chopped

2 tablespoons soy sauce

1 tablespoon finely chopped garlic

1 teaspoon freshly ground black pepper

1 tablespoon sherry

2-3 drops sesame oil

pot sticker wrappers

1 teaspoon peanut oil

⅓ cup water

- Combine chicken, tofu, basil, mushrooms, olives, soy sauce, garlic, pepper, sherry and sesame oil.

- Refrigerate 15 minutes.

- Spread pot sticker wrapper on work surface. Place spoonful of mixture just off center. Bring larger half over. Lightly brush edge of wrapper with water and crimp the two surfaces together.

- Heat peanut oil in large frying pan. Arrange pot stickers in pan and brown on one side. Add water to pan, cover and cook for 3-4 minutes or until all liquid has disappeared. Serve hot with Dipping Sauce.

Dipping Sauce

¼ cup soy sauce

¼ cup vinegar

2 dashes hot chili oil, or to taste

- Combine soy sauce, vinegar and hot chili oil. Adjust to taste.

Yields 3-4 dozen.

To shred meat, take between fingers and tear apart or use a fork.

Caesar Cream Dip

½ cup freshly grated
　　Parmesan cheese
2-3 drained canned anchovy
　　fillets
3 tablespoons lemon juice
½ cup chopped parsley
1 cup light sour cream
1 tablespoon Dijon mustard
3 small cloves garlic
　　assorted fresh vegetables

- In blender or food processor, combine all ingredients except vegetables and purée until smooth.
- Refrigerate at least one hour before serving.
- Serve with cut-up assorted vegetables.

Yields 1½ cups.

48 calories; 3 grams fat; 49% calories from fat; 155 mg. sodium

Vegetable Dip

½ cup plain lowfat yogurt
1 cup lowfat cottage cheese
3 tablespoons chopped
　　chives
2 tablespoons chopped
　　parsley
1 clove garlic, crushed
½ teaspoon salt
1 teaspoon Worcestershire
　　sauce
¼ teaspoon bottled red
　　pepper sauce
　　raw vegetables

- Combine all ingredients except vegetables in blender.
- Refrigerate 2 hours to blend flavors. Serve with raw vegetables.

Yields 12 (2 tablespoon) servings.

Variation: Add 3 tablespoons chopped olives.

21 calories; trace gram fat; 17% calories from fat; 173 mg. sodium

Tapenade

2 cloves garlic
6 flat anchovy fillets, drained
1½ cups pitted Kalamata olives
3 tablespoons bottled capers, drained
½ teaspoon dried rosemary, crumbled
½ teaspoon dried oregano, crumbled
¼ cup olive oil
salt and pepper, to taste
parsley or cilantro, very finely minced, for garnishing
baguette slices

- Combine garlic, anchovies, olives, capers, rosemary, oregano and oil in food processor or blender. Process to coarse grind. Salt and pepper to taste.

- Serve on toasted baguette slices. Garnish with parsley or cilantro.

Yields 1 cup.

Caviar Pie

1 8-ounce package cream cheese
1½ tablespoons mayonnaise
1 jar black caviar
½ lemon
4 hard-boiled eggs, finely chopped
2 bunches green onion, finely chopped
toasted baguettes or mini bagel halves

- Mix together cream cheese and enough mayonnaise to make smooth, creamy consistency. Press into 9-inch pie plate.

- Drain caviar on paper towel.

- Cover with caviar. Sprinkle with freshly squeezed lemon. Cover with eggs and top with onion.

- Serve on baguette slices or bagel halves.

Yields 6 servings.

Parmesan Cheese and Artichoke Dip

6 ounces Parmesan cheese,
  grated
1 cup mayonnaise
2 tablespoons chopped
  onion
1-2 tablespoons lemon juice
1 6-ounce jar marinated
  artichoke hearts, drained
tortilla chips

- Preheat oven to 350°.
- Combine all ingredients except tortilla chips in food processor. Blend until smooth. Pour into small casserole.
- Bake 30 minutes until golden brown on top.
- Serve with tortilla chips.

Yields 6-8 servings.

Scallops with Tomatoes and White Wine

1 pound scallops
flour
salt and pepper
2 tablespoons olive oil
4-6 tablespoons butter,
  divided
1½ teaspoons minced garlic
4 medium tomatoes, peeled,
  seeded and sliced
  lengthwise
1½ tablespoons finely
  chopped fresh basil
1 tablespoon finely chopped
  fresh parsley
½ cup white wine
1-2 teaspoons lemon juice
baguette, diagonally
  sliced, spread with olive
  oil and baked until
  golden brown

- Slice scallops and dust with flour. Season lightly with salt and pepper.
- Heat oil in small pan. When hot, add 2 tablespoons butter. Add scallops and sauté until just opaque, but not fully cooked, about 1 minute. Pour off fat.
- Add garlic to scallops and cook for 30 seconds. Add tomatoes, basil and parsley and toss. Deglaze with white wine and lemon juice. Rapidly whisk in 2-4 tablespoons butter, bit by bit. Sauce should emulsify. Season to taste with salt and pepper.
- Serve on toasted baguette slices.

Yields 4 servings.

Lumpia (Filipino Spring Roll)

Lumpia Sauce

2 green onions, chopped
1-2 large cloves garlic, peeled and run through garlic press
¼ cup soy sauce
¼ cup vinegar
2 tablespoons sugar
2 tablespoons sesame seeds, ground
salt and pepper to taste
Tabasco sauce, optional

- Mix all ingredients together. Set aside.

Lumpia

1 pound ground pork, chicken, shrimp or lean beef
1 clove garlic, minced
½ round onion, minced
1 10-ounce package bean sprouts
1 9-ounce package chop suey mix
1½ teaspoons salt
¼ teaspoon pepper
2 tablespoons flour
¼ cup water
1 16-ounce package frozen lumpia wrappers, thawed
oil for frying

- Brown meat with garlic and onion. Add vegetables and seasonings. Cook 2 minutes. Drain and cool.

- Mix flour and water to create paste. Set aside.

- Place 2 tablespoons of filling on wrapper. Fold nearest edge of wrapper over filling. Fold left and right sides toward center. Roll lightly toward open edge. Seal with paste.

- Heat oil in frying pan. Fry lumpia until golden brown. Drain.

- Serve with lumpia sauce.

Yields 26-28 lumpias.

BREAD & BREAKFAST

Bread & Breakfast

Noel Trainor's Irish Soda Bread

1 cup butter, softened
5¾ cups bread flour
1⅛ cups granulated sugar
2½ cups buttermilk
2 teaspoons salt
3 teaspoons baking powder
3 teaspoons baking soda
2 eggs, beaten
1½ cups raisins

Garnish

melted butter
granulated sugar

- Preheat oven to 350°. Grease 8-inch cake pan.

- Mix butter with dry ingredients. Add eggs and raisins. Mix well.

- Knead dough into a ball. Distribute dough evenly in pan.

- Cut an "X" on top of dough (for releasing steam). Brush top with melted butter. Sprinkle generously with granulated sugar. Allow dough to sit 10 minutes prior to baking.

- Bake 40 minutes. Serve warm or at room temperature.

Yields 6-8 servings.

Banana Muffins

½ cup butter
1 cup sugar
1 egg, beaten
3 bananas, mashed
4 teaspoons milk
½ teaspoon vanilla
1 teaspoon baking soda
½ teaspoon salt
1½ cups flour
½ cup chopped macadamia nuts
¾ cup raisins

- Preheat oven to 350°. Grease and flour muffin tins or use paper muffin cups.

- Cream butter and sugar. Add egg and mix until fluffy. Add bananas, milk and vanilla. Mix well.

- Sift soda, salt and flour together. Add to banana mixture and mix only until dry ingredients are moistened. Add nuts and raisins.

- Bake 20-25 minutes.

Yields 12 muffins.

Chunky Apple Pancakes

2 medium apples
1 cup flour, unsifted
2 teaspoons baking powder
1 teaspoon salt
¼ cup sugar
1 egg
⅓ cup milk
2 teaspoons butter, melted
  Cinnamon Butter

- Preheat electric griddle to 375° or heat stove top griddle over medium-high heat.

- Peel and thinly slice apples. Cut each slice into small pieces.

- In bowl, stir together flour, baking powder, salt and sugar.

- Beat together egg, milk and melted butter. Pour all at once into dry ingredients. Mix until smooth. Add apple pieces.

- Lightly grease preheated griddle. Ladle about ¼ cup batter for each pancake onto griddle. Spread into 4-inch round. Cook until bottoms are browned. Flip and cook other sides. Serve hot with Cinnamon Butter.

Cinnamon Butter

½ cup butter, softened
¼ cup powdered sugar
½ teaspoon ground
   cinnamon

- Cream together butter, powdered sugar and cinnamon.

Yields 8-12 pancakes.

Polenta Rolls

Make in your bread machine.

1⅛ cups water
  3 cups bread flour
  ¾ cup polenta
1½ teaspoons salt
  3 tablespoons sugar
  1 tablespoon plus
    1 teaspoon honey
1½ tablespoons dry milk
  3 tablespoons butter
1½ teaspoons dry yeast
  1 egg, beaten with
    1 teaspoon water

- Place all ingredients into bread pan. Set on dough. When mixing and rising is complete, form 12 balls on lightly-floured surface. Cover rolls and let rest 20 minutes.

- Flatten each ball into wedge shape. Starting with widest side, roll wedge loosely towards point.

- Place on greased baking pan with point on bottom. Spray lightly with water. Let rise until almost double in size (30-40 minutes).

- Preheat oven to 350°.

- Brush rolls with beaten egg. Bake for 10-15 minutes until golden brown.

- Remove from baking pan. Serve warm.

Yields 12 servings.

Variation: Add ¾ cup cubed sharp cheddar cheese and/or 1 teaspoon chili flakes.

184 calories; 4 grams fat; 17% of calories from fat; 326 mg. sodium

Lemon Bread

Bread

¼ cup shortening
1 cup sugar
2 eggs
½ cup milk
1½ cups flour
1½ teaspoons baking powder
½ teaspoon salt
   grated rind of 1 lemon
   Glaze

Glaze

   juice of 1 lemon
½ cup sugar

- Preheat oven to 350°. Grease and flour loaf pan.
- Cream shortening and sugar. Add eggs. Beat. Add milk, flour, baking powder and salt. Fold in lemon rind. Pour batter into loaf pan.
- Bake 45-60 minutes. Remove from oven. Cover hot bread with glaze and allow to soak in.

- Dissolve sugar in lemon juice.

Yields 8-10 servings.

Banana Bread

½ cup butter, softened
1 cup sugar
1¾ cups flour
1 teaspoon baking powder
½ teaspoon salt
2 cups mashed banana
2 eggs, beaten
1 cup walnuts or pecans

- Preheat oven to 350°. Grease and flour loaf pan.
- Cream butter and sugar.
- Combine flour, baking powder and salt. Blend dry ingredients with creamed butter.
- Add mashed banana, eggs and nuts. Pour into prepared pan.
- Bake 1 hour or until tester comes out clean.

Yields 12 servings.

Whole Wheat Zucchini Muffins

¾ cup whole wheat flour
¼ cup all-purpose flour
3 tablespoons sugar
1 teaspoon baking powder
½ teaspoon salt
⅓ cup skim milk
2 egg whites
2 tablespoons vegetable oil
½ teaspoon finely shredded
    orange peel
½ cup shredded zucchini
½ cup chopped nuts

- Preheat oven to 400°. Spray 8 muffin cups with nonstick cooking spray.

- Combine whole wheat flour, all-purpose flour, sugar, baking powder, and salt. Set flour mixture aside.

- Beat together milk, egg whites, oil, and orange peel.

- Add zucchini and nuts to milk mixture.

- Pour wet ingredients into flour mixture. Stir until just moistened. Fill muffin cups ½ full.

- Bake 15-20 minutes until golden brown.

Yields 8 servings.

Giant Herbed Breadsticks

¼ cup butter, softened
¼ cup minced green onion
1 clove garlic, minced
¼ teaspoon dried thyme
1 small baguette

- Preheat broiler.

- Cut baguette lengthwise into quarters.

- Beat together butter, green onion, garlic and thyme. Spread mixture over cut sides of bread. Place bread sticks on baking sheet.

- Broil 4 inches from heat until golden brown.

Yields 2 servings.

Mango Bread

2 cups flour, sifted
2 teaspoons baking soda
1 teaspoon cloves
1 teaspoon allspice
½ teaspoon salt
1½ cups sugar
3 eggs
½ cup vegetable oil
½ cup melted butter
2 cups partly mashed,
   partly diced mangoes
½ cup chopped nuts

- Preheat oven to 350°. Grease and flour 2 loaf pans.
- Combine dry ingredients.
- Beat eggs. Add oil and butter and beat about 2 minutes.
- Add dry ingredients and mangoes alternately. Add nuts. Bake 45-55 minutes.

Yields 2 loaves, 12 servings each.

Zucchini Bread

3 eggs
2 cups sugar
1 cup vegetable oil
1 tablespoon vanilla
2 cups loosely packed,
   grated zucchini
2 cups flour
1 tablespoon cinnamon
1 teaspoon salt
2 teaspoons baking soda
¼ teaspoon baking powder
1 cup chopped walnuts

- Preheat oven to 350°. Grease 2 loaf pans.
- Beat eggs until frothy. Add sugar, oil and vanilla. Beat 1 minute until thick and lemon-colored.
- Stir in zucchini, flour, cinnamon, salt, baking soda and baking powder. Mix well. Fold in walnuts. Spoon into loaf pans.
- Bake 1 hour. Cool in pans 10 minutes before removing.

Yields 2 loaves, 12 servings each.

Winning Malasadas

These classic Portuguese doughnuts are an island favorite.

2 packages dry yeast
1 teaspoon sugar, 1 cup
   sugar, sugar for rolling
   cooked malasadas
⅓ cup warm water
8 cups flour, sifted
1 teaspoon salt
½ cup butter, melted
7 whole eggs
7 egg yolks
1⅓ cups evaporated milk
1⅓ cups water
   vegetable oil for deep
   frying

- Dissolve yeast and 1 teaspoon sugar in warm water. Set aside.

- In large bowl, sift together flour, 1 cup sugar and salt. Add yeast mixture, butter, eggs and egg yolks. Mix with hands in circular motion, squeezing batter through fingers. Set aside.

- Combine evaporated milk and water. Add slowly to batter. Use hands to mix and form soft dough.

- Place in ungreased bowl. Cover and set in warm, draft-free area. Let rise to double in bulk (about 2 hours).

- Punch down and allow to rise about 30 minutes. Set aside.

- In deep-fat fryer, heat oil to 375°. (When oil is hot enough, a small amount of dough will puff up and brown within a few seconds.)

- Shape dough into balls. With thumb, make indentation in ball.

- With spoon, gently drop ball into hot oil. Allow crust to form. Then turn dough over to prevent oil from soaking into uncooked side. Cook a few minutes, until golden brown.

- Drain on paper towels and roll in sugar.

Yields 5 dozen.

Papaya Bread

3 eggs
¾ cup oil
1 cup sugar
1 cup shredded carrots
1½ cups applesauce
1½ cups mashed papaya
1¼ cups chopped walnuts
1 teaspoon salt
4 cups flour
1 tablespoon baking soda
1 tablespoon cinnamon
1 teaspoon nutmeg

- Preheat oven to 325°. Spray 2 loaf pans with nonstick cooking spray.
- Combine eggs, oil and sugar. Mix on low speed for 30 seconds.
- Add carrots, applesauce, papaya puree and nuts. Mix on low speed for another 30 seconds.
- Combine salt, flour, baking soda, cinnamon and nutmeg. Add to wet mixture and mix with light hand, until just combined. Spoon batter into loaf pans.
- Bake 55-60 minutes. Let rest in pan 10 minutes. Cool on wire rack.

Yields 2 loaves, 12 servings each.

233 calories; 12 grams fat; 44% calories from fat; 266 mg. sodium

Pane Toscano (Italian Tuscan Bread)

1 **envelope dry yeast**
½ **teaspoon sugar**
2 **cups warm water (105-115°), divided**
4 **cups unbleached flour**
½ **cup whole wheat flour**

- Sprinkle yeast and sugar over ½ cup warm water. Let stand 5 minutes. Stir to dissolve yeast.

- Add yeast mixture and 1½ cups water to flour. Stir to make soft dough.

- Knead by hand or with electric mixer at low speed 5 minutes until dough is smooth and elastic. Add more flour if needed. Dough should remain somewhat sticky and moist.

- Oil large bowl. Add dough. Oil top of dough by turning once in bowl. Cover with kitchen towel.

- Let stand in warm, draft-free place until double in bulk (about 1½ hours).

- Dust baking sheet with flour. Knead dough briefly to eliminate air bubbles. Cut dough into 2 pieces. Roll each piece by hand to shape into 14-inch loaf. Place loaves on baking sheet several inches apart. Cover loosely with towel. Let rise 30 minutes.

- Preheat oven to 400°.

- Bake 40 minutes until bread is browned and sounds hollow when tapped on bottom. Cool on wire rack.

Yields 30 slices (15 slices per loaf.

68 calories; trace of fat; 3% calories from fat; 1 mg. sodium

Island Muffins

Topping

½ **cup firmly packed brown sugar**
½ **cup coconut**
½ **cup finely chopped macadamia nuts**
¼ **cup butter, melted**

- Combine all ingredients and mix well.

Muffins

2½ **cups flour**
⅓ **cup firmly packed brown sugar**
1 **teaspoon baking soda**
½ **teaspoon salt**
1 **cup sour cream**
⅓ **cup vegetable oil**
1 **egg**
1 **8-ounce can crushed pineapple, undrained**

- Preheat oven to 400°. Generously grease 24 muffin cups.
- In large bowl, mix together flour, brown sugar, baking soda and salt.
- In small bowl, mix together sour cream, oil, egg and pineapple. Blend well.
- Add pineapple mixture to dry ingredients and stir just until moistened.
- Spoon rounded teaspoonful topping into bottom of each muffin cup.
- Spoon tablespoonful batter over topping mix in each muffin cup.
- Bake 12-15 minutes until toothpick inserted in center comes out clean.
- Loosen edges with knife and immediately invert onto wire rack.

Yields 24 muffins.

Ham and Cheese Bake

Makes a wonderful brunch dish as it can be prepared the day before and baked the next morning.

12 slices French bread
6 slices ham
6 slices cheddar cheese
4 eggs, beaten
1 teaspoon dry mustard
½ teaspoon salt
1 quart milk
1 cup grated cheddar
   cheese
paprika
applesauce or spiced
   apples

- Butter 9x13-inch baking pan.
- Make 6 sandwiches with bread, ham and cheese slices. Place in baking pan.
- Combine eggs, mustard, salt and milk. Pour over sandwiches. Sprinkle with grated cheese and paprika.
- Refrigerate at least 1 hour or overnight.
- Preheat oven to 350°.
- Bake 1½ hours.
- Serve with applesauce or spiced apples.

Yields 6 servings.

Corn Bread Casserole

½ cup butter
1 egg
1 cup sour cream
1 15-ounce can creamed
   corn
1 15¼-ounce can corn
   kernels, drained
1 8½-ounce box corn muffin
   mix
salt and pepper, to taste

- Preheat oven to 350°. Lightly grease 2-quart casserole dish.
- Melt butter. Mix with egg and sour cream.
- Add creamed corn, corn kernels, muffin mix, salt and pepper. Mix well. Pour into casserole dish.
- Bake 45 minutes.

Yields 12 servings.

Bread and Cheese Soufflé

For brunch, serve with fresh fruit, toast and home fries. For luncheon or dinner, accompany it with salad or steamed vegetables.

1 **cup milk, hot, scalded**
1 **cup soft bread crumbs**
1 **cup grated cheddar or**
   Swiss cheese
1 **tablespoon butter**
½ **teaspoon salt**
3 **eggs, separated**

- Preheat oven to 350°. Grease 1-quart baking dish.

- Stir bread crumbs, cheese, butter and salt into hot milk. Stir until cheese melts, heating gently if necessary.

- Beat egg yolks. Add cheese mixture gradually to yolks to prevent scrambling eggs.

- Beat egg whites until stiff and fold into cheese mixture.

- Pour into prepared baking dish. Set dish in pan of hot water.

- Bake 30-40 minutes until puffed and golden. Serve immediately.

Yields 4 servings.

Note: Bake in low center of oven so top does not brown before center is cooked.

Buttermilk Pancakes

2 **cups flour**
2 **cups buttermilk**
1 **teaspoon carbonated soda,**
   non-cola
2 **teaspoons baking soda**
1 **teaspoon salt**
2 **tablespoons vegetable oil**
2 **eggs**

- Preheat griddle. (Griddle is correct temperature when cold water drops bounce on surface.) Lightly grease it.

- Mix all ingredients thoroughly.

- Ladle batter onto griddle and cook first side until surface is covered with bubbles. Turn and cook second side until lightly browned.

Yields 16 pancakes.

Tropical Crunch Granola

5 cups old-fashioned rolled oats

1 cup shredded coconut

½ cup macadamia nuts or almonds, coarsely chopped

¼ cup sesame seeds

½ cup sunflower seeds, shelled

½ cup wheat germ, unsweetened

5 tablespoons honey

¼ cup vegetable oil

½ cup dried mango, chopped

½ cup raisins

- Preheat oven to 300°.
- Combine oats, coconut, nuts, sesame seeds, sunflower seeds and wheat germ in large bowl.
- Combine honey and oil. Stir into oat mixture.
- Spread mixture in large pan or roaster.
- Bake 45-50 minutes or until light golden brown. Stir every 15 minutes. Remove from oven.
- Stir in dried mango and raisins. Transfer to another pan to cool. Stir occasionally.

Yields 12 cups.

Note: Store in tightly closed jars or plastic bags. To save for more than 2 weeks, seal and freeze.

185 calories; 9 grams fat; 42% calories from fat; 16 mg. sodium

Eggs MacMillan with Caper and Dill Cream-Cheese Sauce

Serve house guests this quick, easy and delicious brunch dish.

Caper and Dill Cream-Cheese Sauce

1 **cup cream cheese**
½ **cup milk**
1 **teaspoon chopped fresh dill**
2 **tablespoons capers (small ones are best)**
  salt and pepper

- Combine cream cheese and milk in small saucepan over low heat. Stir until warm and smooth. Add dill and capers. Season with salt and pepper. Keep warm over low heat.

4 **English muffins**
8 **slices smoked salmon**
8 **thin slices Maui onion**
8 **poached eggs**
  Caper and Dill Cream-Cheese Sauce
  dill sprigs
  chopped chives

- Preheat broiler.
- Split English muffins with fork and toast under broiler until just brown.
- Put two muffin halves on each plate. Top each half with slice of smoked salmon, slice of onion, poached egg and ¼ cup of sauce. Garnish with sprig of dill and chopped chives.

Yields 4 servings.

Nuts and Berries Granola

7 cups old-fashioned rolled
   oats
1 cup unprocessed bran
1 teaspoon cinnamon
1¼ cups vegetable oil
½ cup honey
½ cup corn syrup
1 teaspoon vanilla
1 cup raw almonds, coarsely
   chopped
1 cup raw pecans, coarsely
   chopped
1 cup dried apricots, cut
   into pieces
1 cup dried cranberries, cut
   coarsely
1 cup mixed dried berries,
   cut coarsely
1 cup raisins

- Preheat oven to 350°.
- Put rolled oats, bran and cinnamon into large roasting or baking pan.
- Mix together oil, honey, corn syrup and vanilla. Pour over dry ingredients and mix well to coat. Spread over bottom of pan.
- Bake 30 minutes, stirring every 10 minutes. Mixture will look browned when done. Cool.
- Toast almonds and pecans until lightly golden. Cool, then break into pieces.
- Add nuts and fruits to oatmeal mixture, stirring well. Store in airtight container. Serve with skim milk or enjoy as snack.

Yields 14 servings.

Variation: Any mix of nuts and berries, more or less than listed, may be used.

One cup of honey equals 1¼ cups granulated sugar. Honey can be substituted in baking, but reduce another liquid proportionally to take into account honey's liquid.

Swedish Pancakes

These crêpe-like pancakes are wonderful for breakfast or brunch.

1⅓ scant cups of milk
3 eggs
1 cup flour
3 tablespoons butter, melted
   jam, fresh fruit or sour cream as topping

- Mix milk, eggs, flour and butter together with beater.

- Heat 8- or 10-inch crêpe or frying pan until very hot.

- Spread ¼ cup batter in frying pan. When pancake bubbles on top, turn over and cook other side. When both sides are lightly browned, remove and serve with topping.

Yields 6-10 servings.

Breakfast Bread Pudding

8 slices bread, crust removed, cut into cubes
1 8-ounce package cream cheese, cut into cubes
12 eggs
2 cups milk
⅓ cup maple syrup, additional syrup
   fresh fruit

- Preheat oven to 375°. Grease 13x9-inch pan.

- Place half of cubed bread in bottom of pan. Cover with cubes of cream cheese. Cover with remaining bread cubes.

- Mix together eggs, milk and maple syrup. Pour over bread mixture. Cover with plastic wrap and refrigerate overnight.

- Bake 45 minutes.

- Serve with maple syrup and fresh fruit.

Yields 8 servings.

Silver Dollar Pancakes

3 eggs
½ teaspoon salt
1 heaping teaspoon baking
   powder
2 cups flour, sifted
2½ cups buttermilk
1 teaspoon baking soda
1 tablespoon melted butter
1 tablespoon warm syrup
   syrup and butter for
      serving

- One hour prior to serving, separate egg whites from yolks. Let whites sit at room temperature. Return yolks to refrigerator.

- Preheat ungreased griddle to 400°.

- Sift together salt, baking powder and flour.

- In separate bowl, combine buttermilk and baking soda. Beat egg yolks and stir into buttermilk mixture. Add flour mixture. Stir lightly to mix. Add butter and syrup. Stir lightly to mix.

- Beat egg whites until soft peaks form. Fold into mixture.

- Drop large tablespoonfuls of batter onto dry, preheated griddle, spreading lightly until each pancake is slightly larger than a silver dollar. Cook until golden brown and air bubbles open and remain open. Turn once.

- Serve on warm platter with warm syrup and melted butter.

Yields 50 pancakes.

Variation: Serve with strawberries and sour cream in place of butter and syrup.

Special Occasion Waffles

1¾ cups flour
3 teaspoons baking powder
½ teaspoon salt
2 egg yolks, beaten
1¼ cups milk
½ cup butter, melted
2 egg whites, beaten stiff

- Preheat waffle iron.
- Sift together dry ingredients.
- Combine egg yolks and milk and stir into dry ingredients. Stir in butter. Gently fold in egg whites. Do not overmix.
- Bake in waffle iron.

Yields 6 servings.

Bagel Croutons

2 plain, whole wheat or
   onion bagels
¼ cup butter
½ teaspoon dried dillweed
⅛ teaspoon garlic or onion
   powder

- Preheat oven to 300°.
- Cut bagels into ¼-inch wedges.
- Melt butter in sauté pan. Add dillweed and garlic or onion powder. Add bagel slices, turning to coat.
- Place bagel slices in a single layer on a cookie sheet. Bake for 10 minutes. Stir. Bake 15 minutes more or until crisp. Let cool.
- Store in airtight container and refrigerate for up to 1 month. Bring to room temperature before tossing with salad.

Yields 2 cups croutons.

per ¼ cup serving:
113 calories; 6 grams fat; 49%
calories from fat; 180 mg. sodium

SOUPS, SALADS & DRESSINGS

Soups, Salads & Dressings

Portuguese Bean Soup

4-5 pieces large, meaty ham
    hocks
1 10-ounce link Portuguese
    sausage
1 large round onion, diced
1 cup diced celery
1 cup diced carrots
2 16-ounce cans stewed
    tomatoes
1 8-ounce can tomato sauce
2 bay leaves
    Worcestershire sauce, to
    taste
    Tabasco sauce, to taste
1 teaspoon sugar
    salt and pepper, to taste
3 tablespoons chopped
    parsley
2 cups cooked elbow
    macaroni
1 15.5-ounce can chili
    beans
1 15-ounce can kidney
    beans
½ small head cabbage,
    chopped

- Bring ham hocks to boil in 1½ gallons of water.
- Simmer until tender, about 2 hours.
- Let meat cool in stock. Remove ham hocks. Refrigerate stock and ham hocks in separate containers overnight.
- Next day, remove fat from stock and ham hocks. Remove meat from ham hocks and dice.
- Dice sausage, place on platter and cover with paper towel. Cook sausage in microwave oven on high about 2 minutes. Wipe off excess fat.
- In large pot, brown Portuguese sausage and onion. Add celery and carrots and sauté 5 minutes.
- Add stock, stewed tomatoes, tomato sauce, bay leaves, Worcestershire sauce, Tabasco sauce, sugar, salt and pepper.
- Bring to boil, then reduce heat. Add parsley, macaroni, chili beans, kidney beans, cabbage and diced ham hock.
- Simmer about 10 minutes.

Yields 20-25 servings.

Lentil-Vegetable Soup

This soup tastes even better when made ahead.

1 large onion, chopped
1 clove garlic, minced
2 tablespoons vegetable oil
3 carrots, sliced
2 stalks celery, sliced
½ teaspoon chili powder
5 cups beef broth (or 6 beef bouillon cubes dissolved in 5 cups water)
1 cup lentils
2 8-ounce cans stewed tomatoes
4-5 cooked red potatoes, cubed
chopped parsley
grated Parmesan cheese

- In large saucepan, cook onion and garlic in oil until limp. Add carrots, celery and chili powder. Cook 1-2 minutes longer, stirring often.
- Add broth and lentils. Cover.
- Simmer until lentils are tender, about 35 minutes. Cool and refrigerate if serving later.
- When ready to serve, add tomatoes and potatoes to reheated soup.
- Ladle into soup bowls. Sprinkle with parsley. Serve with Parmesan cheese.

Yields 2½ quarts or 4-6 servings.

Variation: For more protein, add 3-4 turkey frankfurters.

Chilled Honolulu Cucumber Soup

6 **Japanese cucumbers,**
   peeled and minced

2 **large cloves garlic, peeled**
   and minced

½ **cup finely sliced green**
   onion

   juice of 1 lemon

1 **quart buttermilk**

½ **cup sour cream**

1 **cup plain yogurt**

1½ **tablespoons chopped**
   fresh dill or ¾ teaspoon
   dried dill

1 **teaspoon salt**

¼ **teaspoon freshly ground**
   pepper

½ **cup toasted macadamia**
   nuts, chopped

- Combine cucumbers, garlic, onion, lemon juice, buttermilk, sour cream, yogurt, dill, salt and pepper. Cover.

- Refrigerate 4-24 hours.

- To serve, ladle into chilled soup bowls and sprinkle with nuts.

Yields 6-9 servings.

Note: Japanese cucumbers have few fully developed seeds, which means you don't have to remove them!

Hint: To toast macadamia nuts, toss in cast-iron skillet over medium-high heat 3 minutes or bake on baking sheet in 350° oven 3-5 minutes until they smell toasty. Watch carefully, because once nuts heat through, they burn quite quickly.

217 calories; 13 grams fat; 53% calories from fat; 591 mg. sodium

As a substitute for buttermilk, combine 1 tablespoon lemon juice or vinegar and enough warm milk to make 1 cup (let stand 5-10 minutes before using; it curdles).

Hot and Sour Soup

4 cups clear chicken broth

2 medium carrots, peeled and thinly sliced

2 stalks celery, thinly sliced

1 large clove garlic, peeled and sliced paper thin

1 teaspoon grated ginger root

½ teaspoon paprika

red pepper flakes (add as much or as little "heat" as desired)

2 large, fresh tomatoes, seeds removed and quartered

1 cup julienned shiitake mushrooms

1 cup thinly slivered raw pork

1 tablespoon chopped mint leaves

1 tablespoon chopped cilantro

2 tablespoons fresh lemon juice, or more according to taste

splash of rice wine vinegar, to taste

- In large saucepan, combine broth, carrots, celery, garlic, ginger root, paprika and pepper flakes. Bring to boil, reduce heat to medium and simmer 5 minutes or until carrots are tender-crisp.

- Add tomatoes, mushrooms and pork to soup. Simmer 3 minutes or until mushrooms and tomatoes are heated through and pork is cooked. Stir in mint, cilantro and lemon juice. Adjust seasonings and add vinegar.

Yields 4 servings.

Variation: In place of pork, substitute ½-pound lump crabmeat or 1 cup cooked chicken breast, cut into bite-size pieces.

Hawaiian Black Bean Soup

Both elegant and hearty, this soup will enliven your taste buds while preserving your health.

Soup

1 tablespoon olive oil

1½ cups diced Maui onion, divided

2 teaspoons cumin

½ teaspoon salt

¼ teaspoon freshly ground pepper

28 ounces chopped tomatoes, undrained

2 15-ounce cans black beans, rinsed and drained

28 ounces chicken broth

Cool Creamy-Hot Topping

½ cup chopped cucumber, seeds removed

½ cup chopped avocado

Cool Creamy-Hot Topping

⅔ cup plain yogurt or sour cream

1-2 teaspoons chili water, or 2 fresh jalapeño peppers, seeded and minced

¼ cup cilantro, minced

- Heat oil in large, heavy pot. Add 1 cup onion, cumin, salt and pepper. Cook, stirring, until onion caramelizes.

- Stir in tomatoes, black beans and broth. Cover pot, bring nearly to a boil, reduce heat and simmer gently for 10 - 15 minutes to blend flavors.

- Let mixture cool a little. Spoon out about 2 cups of soup and set aside. Purée remaining mixture, then combine puréed and reserved soup. Heat.

- Ladle soup into individual soup bowls. Spoon topping on each serving. Garnish with ½ cup onion, cucumber and avocado.

- Whisk together yogurt, chili water (or chopped jalapeños) and cilantro.

Yields 8 servings.

Note: This soup can be made as long as 4 days ahead. The topping can be made 2 days ahead.

Pineapple Soup (Vietnamese Sour Soup)

1 pound fresh pineapple
(2½ cups)
1 pound tomatoes (2½ cups)
½ pound medium-size
shrimp
1 pound snapper or
mahimahi
5 green onions, extra
chopped green onion for
garnish
2 teaspoons fish sauce
1 tablespoon tamarind
powder
1 fresh chili, chopped
1 14.5-ounce can chicken
broth
1 broth-can water
2-3 twigs Thai basil for
garnish
chili pepper, to taste

- Cut up pineapple and tomatoes into small pieces.

- Clean, peel and devein shrimp. Cut fish into chunks.

- Cut green onions into 1-inch pieces. Add fish sauce, tamarind powder and fresh chili.

- Put chicken broth and water in large sauce pan. Bring to boil. Add pineapple, tomatoes and fish sauce mixture.

- Simmer 5 minutes. Skim off foam when boiling.

- Bring broth back to boil and add fish and shrimp.

- Cook 3 minutes.

- Serve garnished with basil leaves and green onion.

Yields 6 servings

Miso Soup

3 cups water
¼ cup dried shrimp
½ cup miso, strained
½ block tofu, cubed
(or as much as desired)
2 green onions, chopped

- Boil water and shrimp for 20 minutes and strain. Add miso and bring to boil. Add tofu and green onion and cook for 1-2 minutes. Serve immediately.

Yields 5-6 servings.

Variations: Instead of dried shrimp stock, use 4 cups water, one 0.3-ounce package dashi-no-moto and 6-8 tablespoons miso. Sliced turnips, cubed eggplant, shredded cabbage and other vegetables may be used instead of, or with, tofu.

Split Pea Soup

1 16-ounce package split green peas
14 cups water
6-8 sections of smoked ham hocks
1 cup grated carrots
1 cup grated celery
1 cup finely chopped onion
1 bay leaf
2 tablespoons lemon juice

- Rinse and check split peas for small stones. Combine water, peas and ham hocks in large pot.
- Simmer 2½ hours.
- Remove ham hocks. Skim off excess fat. Add carrots, celery, onions, bay leaf and lemon juice to pot.
- Simmer 30 minutes longer.
- While vegetables are simmering, remove meat from ham hock bones and chop. Be sure to remove all fat. When vegetables are tender, remove bay leaf. Return meat to soup. Heat thoroughly and serve.

Yields 8 servings.

Yogurt Mushroom Soup

¼ **cup butter**
1 **medium onion, chopped**
6 **green onions, sliced**
¾ **pound mushrooms, sliced**
2 **teaspoons paprika**
¼ **cup flour**
6 **cups chicken broth**
2 **egg yolks**
1½ **cups unflavored yogurt**
¼ **teaspoon dried or**
   1 tablespoon finely
   chopped fresh dill

- In three-quart saucepan, melt butter. Add onion and green onions. Cook until limp.
- Add mushrooms and cook, stirring occasionally, until soft.
- Stir in paprika, flour and chicken broth and stir until thick. Cover.
- Simmer 30 minutes.
- Lightly beat egg yolks. Mix in yogurt and dill. Stir about 1 cup of hot broth into egg mixture. Return to soup and stir until thickened over low heat. The soup improves as it sits.

Yields 6-8 servings.

201 calories; 14 grams fat; 60% calories from fat; 1114 mg. sodium

Oyster Stew

24 oysters, chilled (4 8-ounce jars)
2 medium potatoes, peeled and diced
1 large onion, chopped
¾ cup chicken broth
1 clove garlic, minced
½ teaspoon dried thyme, crushed
¼ teaspoon pepper
⅛ teaspoon salt
1 cup whipping cream
¾ cup milk
3 tablespoons dry white wine
   bread or oyster crackers

- Drain oysters, reserving ½ cup liquid; add water, if necessary, to make ½ cup. Cook oysters in that liquid for 3 to 4 minutes, stirring frequently, or until edges of oysters curl. Set aside.

- In large saucepan, combine potatoes, onion, chicken broth, garlic, thyme, pepper and salt. Bring to boil.

- Reduce heat and simmer, covered, about 20 minutes or until potatoes are tender.

- Stir cream and milk into potato mixture. Bring to just boiling.

- Add cooked oysters with their liquid and wine. Heat through, stirring occasionally. Season to taste.

- Ladle into bowls and serve with bread or oyster crackers.

Yields 3-4 servings.

Bread slices easier when partially frozen.

White Chili

1 pound dried Great Northern white beans

2 pounds boneless chicken breasts

1 tablespoon olive oil

2 medium onions, chopped

1 green bell pepper, chopped

4 cloves garlic, minced

2 4-ounce cans chopped mild green chiles

2 teaspoons ground cumin

1½ teaspoons dried oregano, crumbled

¼ teaspoon ground cloves

¼ teaspoon cayenne pepper

6 cups chicken stock or canned broth

3 cups grated Monterey Jack cheese, divided

salt and pepper, to taste

sour cream

salsa

chopped fresh cilantro

- Pick over and rinse beans. Pour beans into large heavy pot and cover with 3 inches cold water. Soak overnight. (Alternatively: Cover with water, bring to boil. Simmer 2 minutes. Cover and let sit 1 hour.) Proceed with recipe.

- Place chicken in large skillet or saucepan. Cover with cold water. Bring to boil. Turn heat down and simmer until tender, about 15 minutes. Drain and cool. Remove skin and cut chicken into cubes. Refrigerate until ready to use.

- Drain beans. In same pot, heat oil. Add onions and sauté until translucent. Stir in bell pepper, garlic, chiles, cumin, oregano, cloves and cayenne and sauté 2 minutes.

- Add beans and stock and bring to boil.

- Reduce heat and simmer until beans are very tender, 1-2 hours.

- At this point, chili can be covered and refrigerated for up to a day. Reheat to simmer.

- To simmering chili, add cubed chicken and 1 cup cheese. Season with salt and pepper.

(Continued)

(White Chili, continued)

- Ladle chili into serving bowls. Garnish each serving with remaining grated cheese, sour cream, salsa and cilantro.

Yields 8 servings.

Note: Don't add salt to cooking liquid before beans are soft. Salt inhibits this process.

Fresh Cream of Asparagus Soup

1 **pound fresh asparagus**
¼ **cup chopped onion**
2 **cups chicken broth, divided**
2 **tablespoons butter**
2 **tablespoons flour**
½ **teaspoon salt**
   dash pepper
1 **cup milk**
½ **cup sour cream or plain yogurt**
1 **tablespoon fresh lemon juice**
   fresh chives for garnish
   Tabasco sauce

- Snap off ends of asparagus. Discard. Peel and chop stalks.

- Cook asparagus, onion, and 1 cup chicken broth in covered saucepan until asparagus is just tender. Press through food mill or blend until smooth.

- Heat butter, flour, salt and pepper in saucepan. Stir in second cup chicken broth. Cook over medium heat, stirring constantly, until mixture reaches boiling point. Mix in asparagus purée and milk.

- Stir a little of this hot mixture into sour cream or yogurt, then stir that back into hot mixture. Add lemon juice.

- Heat just to serving temperature, stirring frequently. Sprinkle with fresh chives for garnish. Offer Tabasco sauce at table.

Yields 4 servings.

Roasted Eggplant and Red Bell Pepper Soup

3 medium eggplants, firm to touch
1 teaspoon olive oil
2 tablespoons olive oil
2 medium red onions, thinly sliced
⅓ cup minced shallots
2 cups thinly sliced red bell pepper
3½ tablespoons minced garlic
2 quarts chicken stock
3 cups peeled, seeded and diced tomatoes, fresh or canned
½ teaspoon chopped fresh thyme
2 tablespoons chopped, fresh basil
½ teaspoon fennel seeds
½ teaspoon red pepper flakes
salt and pepper
sour cream for garnish

- Preheat oven to 450°. Spread 1 teaspoon oil on baking sheet.

- Slice eggplants (unpeeled) into rounds and lay on baking sheet.

- Heat remaining 2 tablespoons oil in sauté pan and sauté onions, shallots, bell peppers and garlic until soft but not brown, about 6 minutes. Spread on top of eggplant rounds.

- Roast 15-20 minutes until eggplant is soft and topping is toasted brown.

- In food processor, process eggplant mixture with stock, tomatoes and seasonings until well blended but not puréed. Remove any large pieces of eggplant skin.

- Gently reheat and correct seasoning. Ladle thick soup into bowls and garnish with sour cream.

Yields 6 servings.

202 calories; 9 grams fat; 36% calories from fat; 1352 mg. sodium

Gazpacho

Prepare this when summer fruit and vegetables are at their peak of flavor.

2 large tomatoes, peeled, divided
1 large cucumber, pared and halved
1 medium sweet onion, peeled and halved
1 medium green bell pepper, quartered and seeded
1 pimento
3 cups tomato juice, divided
4 tablespoons olive oil, divided
⅓ cup red wine vinegar
¼ teaspoon Tabasco, or more, to taste
1 teaspoon salt
⅛ teaspoon freshly ground pepper
2 cloves garlic, split
½ cup bread cubes
¼ cup chopped chives

- In blender, purée one tomato, cucumber half, onion half, green-pepper quarter, pimento and ½ cup tomato juice.

- Mix puréed vegetables with 2½ cups tomato juice, 2 tablespoons olive oil, vinegar, Tabasco, salt and pepper.

- Coarsely chop remaining tomato, cucumber, onion and green pepper. Add to puréed mixture.

- Refrigerate at least 2 hours.

- Rub inside of small skillet with cut garlic. (Reserve garlic.) Add 2 tablespoons olive oil. Heat. Sauté bread cubes until browned. Set aside until serving time.

- Before serving, crush reserved garlic and add to soup. Mix well. Adjust seasonings, adding more Tabasco, salt, pepper, oil or vinegar if desired. Ladle into chilled soup bowls and sprinkle with chopped chives. Serve with browned bread cubes.

Yields 6 servings.

Note: A pinch of sugar will counter-act acidity, if necessary.

Good to Go Roasted Corn Chowder

2 pounds fresh corn kernels
1 teaspoon salt
1 teaspoon white pepper
6 tablespoons vegetable oil
1½ cups finely diced onion
2 cloves garlic, minced
1½ cups finely diced celery
¾ cup finely diced green bell pepper
¾ cup finely diced red bell pepper
3 ounces tomato paste (½ of 6-ounce can)
6 ounces all-purpose flour (about 1½ cups)
2 quarts low fat, low sodium, chicken stock, heated
3 bay leaves
1 tablespoon thyme leaves, fresh or dried
2 pounds russet potatoes, peeled, medium dice, reserved in water
⅓ cup finely diced sun-dried tomatoes
3 cups skim milk, heated
1 cup heavy cream, heated
4 tablespoons Worcestershire sauce
1 tablespoon Tabasco

- Preheat oven to 350°. Prepare cookie sheet with nonstick cooking spray.
- Roast corn by spraying kernels with nonstick cooking spray and toss with salt and pepper. Place on cookie sheet.
- Roast for 30 minutes.
- Purée ¾ of cooled corn in food processor; reserve with remaining kernels.
- Heat 7-quart, heavy-gauge pot. Add oil and sauté onions until translucent.
- Add garlic, celery and bell peppers, sautéing until heated through. Add tomato paste. On high heat, stir constantly until mixture browns.
- Turn off heat and stir in flour until fully incorporated (about 5 minutes).
- Place pot back on heat and whisk in hot chicken stock. Bring to boil; reduce heat and add bay leaves, thyme, potatoes, corn and sun-dried tomatoes.
- Simmer about 1 hour until potatoes are tender. Remove bay leaves.
- Add hot skim milk and cream. Adjust seasonings with salt, white pepper, Worcestershire sauce and Tabasco.

Yields 16 12-ounce servings.

Cold Apricot Soup

12 apricots, peeled and
    pitted
1 cup dried California
    apricots
4 cups orange juice
4 peeled kiwis
½ cup honey
⅛ teaspoon freshly grated
    nutmeg
    mint leaves for garnish

- Place ¼ of fresh and dried apricots, orange juice, kiwis and honey into blender and process. Pour through sieve into large bowl or container.
- Add any dried apricots remaining in sieve to next batch.
- Repeat with quarter amounts until all blended. Refrigerate one hour or overnight.
- Serve in chilled bowls. Float three mint leaves in center as garnish.

Yields about eight cups.

208 calories; 1 fat gram; 3% calories from fat; 6 mg. sodium

Cold Zucchini Soup

Refreshing and delicious on a hot day.

5 small to medium
    zucchini, cubed
4 cups water
1 teaspoon curry powder
4 chicken bouillon cubes
3 ounces light cream cheese

- Cook zucchini in water with curry powder and bouillon cubes until tender. Do not drain. Put in blender by cupfuls. Purée. Add cream cheese gradually. Serve cold.

Yields 1½ quarts.

"Super" Salad

1 head cauliflower florets
1 head broccoli florets
4 ounces cheddar cheese, grated
½ pound bacon, cooked and crumbled
1 green bell pepper, chopped
1 small onion, chopped
Dressing

- Mix salad ingredients together and stir in dressing. Best if made a day ahead.

Dressing

1 cup sour cream
1 cup mayonnaise-type salad dressing
¼ cup sugar

- Mix all ingredients together until well blended.

Yields 6-8 servings.

Spinach Salad Dressing

1 cup olive oil
⅓ cup ketchup
⅔ cup sugar
1 tablespoon Worcestershire sauce
¼ cup red wine vinegar
¼ teaspoon salt
¼ teaspoon pepper
¼ cup minced Maui onion

- Combine all ingredients. Mix well.

Yields about 3 cups.

'Ono Salad Dressing

Use this 'ono (delicious) dressing for fresh or cooked vegetables or as marinade for shrimp.

1 clove garlic, mashed
1 cup salad oil
½ cup sugar
½ cup Japanese rice vinegar
2 teaspoons salt
½ teaspoon pepper
¼ cup mayonnaise
1 teaspoon dry mustard

- Mix ingredients in blender and chill.

Yields 2 cups.

Variation: As a marinade for fresh shrimp, wash shrimp, remove legs, and soak (with shells on) in dressing overnight. Grill over coals.

Mandarin Orange Salad

Salad

2 tablespoons sugar
¼ cup sliced almonds
1 head lettuce, shredded
1 cup chopped celery
1 tablespoon chopped parsley
2 tablespoons chopped green onion
1 11-ounce can mandarin orange segments, drained
Dressing

- Melt sugar in small skillet over low heat. Add almonds and caramelize until brown. Cool on foil or waxed paper. Break apart.

- Toss together lettuce, celery, parsley, green onion and oranges. Add dressing and gently combine. Sprinkle almonds on top.

Dressing

2 tablespoons rice wine vinegar
2 tablespoons sugar
¼ cup vegetable oil
12 drops Tabasco sauce

- Mix vinegar, sugar, oil and Tabasco. Shake well.

Yields 6 servings.

Salmon and Cucumber Salad

Salad

1 Japanese cucumber
1 cup cold cooked salmon
(poached or grilled),
flaked
4 cups Manoa lettuce or
other greens, torn into
bite-size pieces
Cucumber Dressing

- Peel skin off cucumber in long strips, leaving ½ of strips on so cucumber is striped. Cut into ⅛-inch slices. Toss cucumber and salmon with lettuce. Add dressing and serve.

Cucumber Dressing

1 Japanese cucumber,
unpeeled
½ cup sour cream
¼ cup mayonnaise
¼ cup finely chopped Maui
onion
2 teaspoons white vinegar
2 tablespoons minced
cilantro
salt and pepper, to taste

- Grate cucumber or slice it into pieces and blend in food processor. Drain in sieve for an hour until liquid is released.
- Combine cucumber with sour cream, mayonnaise, onion, vinegar, cilantro, salt and pepper.

Yields 4 servings of salad; 1 cup of dressing.

Walnut Gorgonzola Salad

1 cup walnuts
2 tablespoons butter
1 tablespoon sugar
1 pound mixed greens such
as baby romaine and
watercress
⅓ cup olive oil
¼ cup balsamic vinegar
salt and pepper
1 cup Gorgonzola cheese

- Sauté walnuts in butter about 5 minutes. Sprinkle with sugar and sauté 1-2 minutes until walnuts are crisp. Cool.
- Toss mixed greens with olive oil to lightly coat them. Drizzle balsamic vinegar over greens, and add salt and pepper to taste.
- Toss with Gorgonzola cheese and walnuts.

Yields 8 servings.

Island Chicken Salad

3 pounds boneless, skinless chicken breasts
1 cup thinly sliced celery
¼ cup thinly sliced green onion
  salt and pepper, to taste
  Dressing
2-3 papayas
¼ cup chopped macadamia nuts

- Steam chicken until just tender. Cool. Cut into cubes.
- Toss cubed chicken with celery and onions. Add salt and pepper to taste.
- Pour dressing over chicken mixture and toss. Cover and refrigerate overnight.
- To serve, cut papayas in half and scoop out seeds. Spoon chicken into papaya halves and garnish with macadamia nuts.

Dressing

1 cup mayonnaise
½ cup sour cream
¼ cup mango chutney
1 tablespoon curry powder
1 tablespoon powdered ginger
½ teaspoon salt

- Combine all ingredients. Mix well.

Yields 4 to 6 servings.

Variation: Add golden raisins or sliced water chestnuts.

Vinegar Garlic Dressing

1⅓ cups vegetable oil
⅔ cup white vinegar
1 tablespoon sugar
2 teaspoons salt
½ teaspoon pepper
1 teaspoon dry mustard
1 clove garlic, crushed

- Combine oil, vinegar, sugar, salt, pepper and mustard in pint bottle. Shake well. Add crushed garlic clove.

Yields 6 servings.

Curried Chicken Salad

1 cup chicken broth
2 tablespoons mirin
2 chicken breast halves
　lemon juice to preserve
　fruit color
2 unpeeled red apples, diced
　and sprinkled with
　lemon juice
1 stalk celery, chopped
1 small Maui onion,
　chopped (about ½ cup)
1 carrot, grated
¼ cup chopped walnuts
¼ cup raisins
2 tablespoons mayonnaise
　(substitute combination
　of mayonnaise and non-
　fat yogurt, if preferred)
2-3 tablespoons chutney
2 teaspoons curry powder
　salt and pepper, to taste
3 papayas
5 lettuce leaves

- Combine chicken broth, mirin and chicken breasts in sauce-pan. Cook chicken until done. Cool. Save remaining liquid.

- After chicken has cooled, dis-card skin and bones. Dice chicken. Pour reserved liquid over chicken and refrigerate for a few hours or overnight. Liquid will be absorbed by chicken pieces. (If serving salad right away, do not use liquid as it will make salad watery. Save for soup stock.)

- Put diced chicken in large bowl. Add apples, celery, onion, car-rot, walnuts and raisins. Stir in mayonnaise, chutney, curry powder, salt and pepper. Re-frigerate until ready to serve.

- Cut papayas in half. Scoop out seeds. Peel skin and cut into strips lengthwise, stopping ½-inch from the end, and fan out fruit.

- Place lettuce leaf, papaya fan and scoop of chicken salad on plate.

Yields 6 servings.

Variation: Cantaloupe, honeydew, mango, peach or nectarine may be substituted for papaya. Toss peach and nectarine in lemon juice to preserve color.

Cashew-Apple Salad

½ **head romaine lettuce**
½ **cup sliced cashews**
½ **cup diced Swiss cheese**
½ **unpeeled red apple,
   chopped**
   Dressing

- Combine lettuce, cashews, cheese and apple. Toss with dressing and serve.

Dressing

½ **cup vegetable oil**
⅙ **cup red wine vinegar**
¼ **cup sugar**
½ **teaspoon Dijon mustard**
1 **teaspoon diced onion**
1-2 **teaspoons poppy seeds
   (add at last minute)**

- Mix ingredients in blender.

Yields 4 servings.

Variation: Substitute almonds for cashews.

Mozzarella and Tomato Salad

½ **pound arugula**
4 **vine-ripened tomatoes,
   sliced**
2 **cups (or one small
   grocer's box) yellow pear
   tomatoes, halved**
8 **ounces fresh mozzarella,
   sliced**
1 **tablespoon thinly sliced
   fresh basil**
10 **Kalamata olives,
   quartered**
2 **tablespoons capers
   balsamic vinegar
   extra virgin olive oil
   salt and freshly ground
   pepper**

- Place arugula on serving plate. Layer tomatoes and mozzarella on greens. Top with basil, olives and capers.
- Drizzle with vinegar and olive oil. Season to taste with salt and pepper.

Yields 8 servings.

Asparagus with Red Pepper Vinaigrette

Especially good for holiday buffet tables.

2 pounds asparagus
1 red bell pepper, chopped,
   for garnish
   Vinaigrette

- Steam asparagus for 5 minutes until crisp-tender. Do not over-cook.

- Arrange asparagus on serving platter and drizzle with vinaigrette. Garnish with chopped red pepper.

Vinaigrette

2 cloves garlic
1 shallot
3 tablespoons chopped red
   bell pepper
2 tablespoons red wine
   vinegar
1 tablespoon balsamic
   vinegar
2 teaspoons fresh lemon
   juice
½ teaspoon salt
¼ teaspoon pepper
2 tablespoons chopped fresh
   basil
½ cup olive oil

- Combine garlic, shallot and red pepper in food processor. Process until finely chopped.

- Add red wine vinegar, balsamic vinegar, lemon juice, salt, pepper and basil. Blend.

- With food processor running, add oil slowly until well blended. Add up to ¼ cup more oil as needed.

Yields 6-8 servings.

Chicken Salad Provençal

2 pounds chicken breasts
¼ cup diced onion
¼ cup diced carrot
¼ cup diced celery
1 bay leaf
  water or chicken stock
⅓ pound green beans
2 Roma tomatoes
4 cups mixed salad greens
2 tablespoons capers
  Vinaigrette
¼ pound aged ricotta or
  mild feta cheese
¼ cup marinated olives
  fresh oregano leaves, torn

- Place chicken, onion, carrot, celery and bay leaf in pot and cover with water or chicken stock. Bring to boil, skimming off any foam from surface. Cover and turn off heat.

- Let stand 45 minutes before removing cover. Let chicken cool in liquid. Remove and chill. (Broth may be used later as thin stock for making risotto or soup.)

- Parboil beans until just tender. Transfer to bowl of ice water to stop cooking. Drain and cut into 1-inch lengths. Halve tomatoes lengthwise and remove core. Cut tomato into lengthwise slices.

- Skin and debone chicken. Remove any fat and gristle. Shred meat by hand.

- Combine chicken, beans, tomatoes, greens and capers in large salad bowl. Add vinaigrette dressing and toss to coat evenly.

- Transfer to individual plates, top with crumbled cheese, olives and oregano.

Vinaigrette

2 tablespoons or juice of
  1 lemon
⅓ cup olive oil
2 teaspoons minced shallots
½ teaspoon dried oregano
  salt and pepper

- In small bowl, combine all ingredients and stir to dissolve salt. Pour over salad.

Yields 4 servings.

Note: This may be used as an entrée or an antipasto.

Fatoosh (Syrian Salad)

1 cup chopped romaine
  lettuce
1 cup diced tomatoes
1 cup diced yellow, red and
  green bell peppers
½ cup finely diced red onion
¼ cup chopped green onion
¼ cup chopped parsley
1 cup chopped mint
  olive oil
  juice of ½ to 1 lemon
3 tablespoons red wine
  vinegar
  salt and pepper
6-8 rounds of toasted pita
  bread

• Mix lettuce, tomatoes, peppers, onions, parsley and mint in salad bowl.

• Coat salad ingredients with oil.

• Add lemon juice and wine vinegar gradually while tossing salad. Add salt and pepper to taste. Serve in pita rounds.

Yields 6-8 servings.

256 calories; 8 grams fat; 27% calories from fat; 337 mg. sodium

Cranberry Salad

2 cups fresh cranberries
1 orange, partially peeled
1 cup sugar
1 3-ounce package lemon
  gelatin
1 tablespoon lemon juice
1 cup boiling water
2 8-ounce cans crushed
  pineapple, drained
  lettuce, mayonnaise and
  paprika for garnish

• Grind cranberries and orange together. Set aside.

• Dissolve sugar and gelatin in lemon juice and water. Chill to partially set.

• After gelatin is partially set, fold in cranberry mixture and pineapple. Pour into 6-cup ring mold or individual molds. Chill to firmly set.

• When ready to serve, unmold on bed of lettuce. Top with dab of mayonnaise. Sprinkle paprika on top.

Yields 10-12 servings.

Chicken Cabbage Salad (Vietnamese style)

1 3-pound chicken
½ cup white vinegar
2 teaspoons sugar
½ teaspoon salt
pepper, to taste
1 small head cabbage, thinly shredded
1 bunch cilantro, finely chopped
1 small Maui onion, thinly sliced
1 carrot, shredded
rau ram (Vietnamese herb), optional

- Boil whole chicken. Let cool. Discard skin, bones and fat, and shred meat.

- Mix vinegar, sugar, salt and pepper.

- When ready to serve, pour half of vinegar mixture on cabbage and toss well. Then add chicken, cilantro, onion, carrot and rau ram. Pour remaining dressing on salad and toss again.

Yields 6-8 servings.

Variation: Substitute torn mint leaves for rau ram.

Minted Tomato-Zucchini Salad

Prepare this salad when tomatoes are bursting with flavor.

4 cups shredded zucchini
½ teaspoon salt
½ cup unflavored yogurt
1-2 tablespoons cider vinegar, to taste
1½ teaspoons sugar
3 tablespoons chopped fresh mint leaves
½ cup thinly sliced green onion, including tops
salt and pepper, to taste
red lettuce leaves, washed
2 large tomatoes, thickly sliced

- Mix zucchini and salt. Let stand 15 minutes. Drain and press out liquid. Pat with paper towel to extract final juice.

- Mix yogurt, vinegar, sugar and mint until well blended. Add onion, zucchini, salt and pepper.

- Arrange lettuce leaves on individual salad plates. Place tomato slice on lettuce and cover with large spoonful of yogurt-zucchini mixture.

Yields 6-8 servings.

Apple Celery Slaw

½ **cup plain low-fat yogurt**
3 **teaspoons sugar**
1 **teaspoon prepared mustard**
½ **teaspoon salt**
 pepper, to taste
1 **medium apple, chopped**
½ **small carrot, shredded**
½ **small stalk celery, thinly sliced**
1½ **cups shredded cabbage**
1 **tablespoon sliced green onion**

- In medium bowl, stir together yogurt, sugar, mustard, salt and pepper. Add apple and stir to coat thoroughly.
- Add carrot, celery, cabbage and green onion. Toss lightly. Cover.
- Chill one hour.

Yields 4 servings.

Black Bean and Tomato Salad

1 **15-ounce can garbanzo beans, drained and rinsed**
1 **15-ounce can black beans, drained and rinsed**
3 **medium tomatoes, seeded and chopped (1½ cups)**
⅓ **cup fresh basil, snipped**
⅓ **cup fresh oregano, snipped**
2 **green onions, sliced**
1 **clove garlic, minced**
½ **teaspoon salt**
¼ **teaspoon pepper**
 fresh oregano sprigs for garnish

- In medium bowl, mix together beans, tomatoes, basil, oregano, green onion, garlic, salt and pepper.
- Let stand at room temperature 30 minutes to 2 hours for flavors to blend.
- Garnish with oregano sprigs, if desired.

Yields 4 servings.

Variation: Combine other canned beans for color and taste variety.

156 calories; 3 grams fat; 14% calories from fat; 706 mg. sodium

Jicama Salad with Cilantro Dressing

Salad

**1 head of romaine lettuce
(or favorite salad greens)**

**1 cucumber, peeled, seeded
and shaved lengthwise
into very thin strips**

**4 carrots, peeled and
shaved lengthwise into
very thin strips**

**12 ounces jicama, peeled
and cut into thin strips
(about 3 cups)**

Cilantro Dressing

- Arrange salad greens on 4 salad plates. Top with cucumber, carrots and jicama. Drizzle dressing over top.

Cilantro Dressing

**1 small Maui onion,
quartered**

¼ cup cilantro leaves

**3 tablespoons white wine
vinegar**

**1 tablespoon lime or lemon
juice**

⅛ teaspoon salt

½ teaspoon pepper

3 tablespoons olive oil

⅓ cup plain fat-free yogurt

- In food processor, place onion, cilantro, vinegar, lime or lemon juice, salt and pepper. Process until combined. With motor running, drizzle in oil until well blended. Stir in yogurt.

Yields 4 servings.

Irresistible Rice and Bean Salad

1 slice bacon, chopped
1 teaspoon reserved bacon drippings or 1 teaspoon vegetable oil
1 cup chopped Maui onion
1 14½-ounce can reduced-sodium chicken broth
¾ cup brown rice, uncooked
1 cup sliced celery
¼ teaspoon salt
¼ teaspoon Tabasco sauce
¼ teaspoon freshly ground black pepper
1 15½-ounce can dark red kidney beans, undrained
½ cup green bell pepper, cut into bite-size pieces

- Cook bacon until crisp. Drain on paper towel.
- Cook onion in drippings until tender. Add bacon, broth, rice, celery, salt, Tabasco and pepper. Bring to boil. Reduce heat.
- Simmer 40 minutes.
- Add beans and green pepper. Simmer, covered, 5 minutes. Serve immediately.

Yields 6 servings.

Tangy Citrus Salad

4 teaspoons Dijon mustard
4 teaspoons freshly squeezed orange juice
2 teaspoons white-wine vinegar
salt and pepper, to taste
¼ cup olive oil
½ pound Nalo greens or mixed baby greens
orange, tangerine, grapefruit, lemon and lime segments, assorted
2 tomatoes, chopped and seeded
fresh chives, chopped

- Whisk together mustard, orange juice, vinegar, salt and pepper. Whisk in oil in steady stream until thickened.
- Place Nalo greens on individual salad plates. Arrange citrus segments attractively on top. Drizzle with dressing and garnish with tomatoes and chives.

Yields 4 servings.

Note: Nalo greens are grown in Waimanalo, Hawaii.

Warm Chicken Salad with Homemade Plum Sauce

Chicken Salad

2 teaspoons peanut oil
4 boneless, skinless chicken breast halves (about 1 pound)
4 cups shredded won bok
1 cup bean sprouts
1 tablespoon thinly sliced green onion
Homemade Plum Sauce

- Heat oil in skillet over medium heat. Cook chicken breasts about 10 minutes, until done.

- Arrange won bok, bean sprouts and onion on 4 serving plates. Slice chicken across grain and fan out on top of vegetables. Spoon plum sauce over chicken.

Homemade Plum Sauce

1 16-ounce can purple plums, rinsed, drained and pitted
1 tablespoon lemon juice
2 teaspoons brown sugar
½ teaspoon grated ginger
⅛ teaspoon crushed red pepper
1 clove garlic

- Put plums, lemon juice, brown sugar, ginger, red pepper and garlic in food processor and blend on high speed until smooth. Heat sauce if desired.

Yields 4 servings.

227 calories; 4 grams fat; 15% calories from fat; 90 mg. sodium

Fruit Salad with Creamy Ginger Dressing

Exact amounts and variety of fruit can vary. Choose brightest, freshest fruit available.

Fruit Mix

1 **medium cantaloupe, cubed**

1 **medium orange, peeled and sectioned**

1 **cup blueberries**

1 **cup halved strawberries**

1 **medium apple, cored and coarsely chopped**

1 **medium nectarine, peeled, pitted and thinly sliced**

juice of 1 lemon mixed with some water

lettuce leaves

Creamy Ginger Dressing

- Combine fruit and toss with mixture of lemon juice and water to prevent darkening.
- Serve fruit on lettuce and top with dressing.

Creamy Ginger Dressing

1 **8-ounce carton peach yogurt (or flavor of choice)**

2 **tablespoons mayonnaise**

2 **teaspoons brown sugar**

1 **teaspoon grated ginger root or ¼ teaspoon ground ginger**

- Stir together all ingredients.

Yields 4 servings.

255 calories; 7 grams fat; 23% calories from fat; 91 mg. sodium

Island Fruit Salad

1 banana, cut up
2 tablespoons pineapple
   juice
1 medium papaya, seeded,
   peeled and sliced
1 medium mango, seeded,
   peeled and sliced
2 cups honeydew and/or
   cantaloupe balls
¼ cup toasted coconut
   fresh mint sprigs

- Combine banana and pine-apple juice in food processor. Blend until smooth.
- Refrigerate while preparing other fruit.
- Arrange papaya and mango on 4 salad plates. Mound ½ cup melon on each plate.
- Spoon banana and pineapple dressing over each and sprinkle with toasted coconut.
- Garnish with mint sprigs and serve.

Yields 4 servings.

Hint: Toast coconut in a 350° oven for 5-10 minutes or until light golden brown. Stir once or twice.

Spinach Salad with Strawberries and Kiwis

2 tablespoons strawberry or
   raspberry vinegar
2 tablespoons strawberry or
   raspberry jam
⅓ cup vegetable oil
1 bunch spinach, torn into
   bite-size pieces
1 pint fresh strawberries,
   halved, or fresh
   raspberries
2 kiwis, peeled and sliced

- In small bowl, whisk together vinegar and jam. Pour oil in steady stream, whisking constantly.
- Place spinach leaves on individual salad plates. Arrange strawberries and kiwi on the top and drizzle with dressing. Serve immediately.

Yields 3-4 servings.

Chicken Salad with Ginger Dressing

Ginger Dressing

⅓ **cup vegetable oil**
¼ **cup white wine vinegar**
1 **tablespoon sugar**
2 **teaspoons soy sauce**
½ **teaspoon pepper**
½ **teaspoon ground ginger**
¼ **teaspoon salt**

- Shake all ingredients together in tightly-closed container. Prepare at least two hours before serving and refrigerate.

Salad

vegetable oil for deep frying
1 **3.75-ounce package rice sticks**
4 **cups Manoa lettuce**
3 **cups diced cooked chicken**
1 **large carrot, shredded**
4 **green onions, including tops, sliced**
1 **tablespoon sesame seed, toasted**
cilantro

- Pour oil to 1-inch in depth in Dutch oven. Heat to 425°. Drop ¼ of rice sticks into hot oil and fry 5 seconds, turning once, until puffed and crisp. Remove immediately from oil, so rice sticks stay white. Drain. Repeat process.

- Toss half of crisp rice sticks, lettuce, chicken, carrot and green onions in large salad bowl. Add ginger dressing and toss again.

- To serve, place remaining crisp rice sticks on large serving platter. Top with salad mixture and garnish with sesame seeds and cilantro. Serve at once.

Yields 6 servings.

Chicken and Soba Noodle Salad

4 **boneless, skinless chicken breast halves**
2 **cloves garlic, minced**
2 **tablespoons freshly grated ginger root**
5 **tablespoons rice vinegar, divided**
1½ **cups chopped fresh cilantro, 4 sprigs for garnish**
⅓ **cup chopped fresh flat leaf parsley**
½ **cup vegetable oil**
¼ **teaspoon red pepper flakes**
3½ **quarts water**
½ **pound dried soba noodles**
1 **cup mung bean sprouts**
3 **green onions, thinly sliced**
1 **carrot, julienned**

- Combine chicken, garlic, ginger root and 1 tablespoon vinegar in sealable bag.

- Marinate 1 hour in refrigerator.

- Preheat grill.

- Discard marinade and grill chicken 4 minutes on each side until just cooked through.

- In blender, purée cilantro, parsley and oil until smooth. Stir in 4 tablespoons vinegar and red pepper flakes. Set dressing aside.

- Boil water and cook noodles 2 minutes until tender but not limp. Do not overcook. Drain and place noodles on serving platter.

- Slice chicken into ½-inch slices. Top noodles with chicken, sprouts, onions and carrot. Drizzle cilantro dressing over all. Garnish with cilantro. Serve immediately.

Yields 4 servings.

Chicken Salad with Fresh Oranges

2 tablespoons finely chopped green onion

2 tablespoons fresh lime juice

¾ teaspoon salt, divided

2½ cups cubed, cooked chicken breasts

1½ cups cooked green peas

1 cup mayonnaise

⅓ cup finely chopped carrot

⅓ cup finely chopped celery

⅓ cup finely snipped, fresh cilantro leaves

3 tablespoons fresh orange juice

½ teaspoon ground cinnamon

¼ teaspoon freshly ground pepper

Manoa or other lettuce

3 navel oranges, peeled and sectioned, membranes removed

2 avocados, peeled and cut into wedges

- Sprinkle green onion with lime juice and ¼ teaspoon salt. Refrigerate covered.

- Combine chicken, peas, mayonnaise, carrot, celery, cilantro, orange juice, ½ teaspoon salt, cinnamon and pepper.

- Refrigerate, covered, at least 1 hour.

- To serve, place lettuce on individual salad plates. Spoon chicken mixture onto lettuce. Garnish with orange and avocado. Sprinkle with chopped green onion.

Yields 6 servings.

Broccoli Salad

Try this sweet and crunchy salad.

1 cup mayonnaise

⅓ cup sugar

1½ tablespoons rice vinegar

1 large bunch broccoli

1 medium red onion, finely chopped

10 slices bacon, fried crisp and crumbled

¾ cup salted sunflower seeds

- Mix mayonnaise, sugar and rice vinegar. Refrigerate overnight.

- Break off broccoli florets and chop finely.

- Mix broccoli, onion, bacon and sunflower seeds. Add dressing before serving.

Yields 6-8 servings.

Chicken and Sugar Snap Pea Pasta Salad

1 8-ounce package spiral macaroni
1 cup fresh sugar snap peas
⅓ cup mayonnaise or salad dressing
¼ cup French dressing
2 cups cooked, diced chicken breast
1 cup cherry tomatoes, halved

- Cook macaroni according to package directions. Add sugar snap peas 1 - 2 minutes before macaroni is done. Drain. Rinse with cold water. Drain.
- Mix mayonnaise and French dressing in large bowl. Add macaroni mixture, chicken and tomatoes. Toss.

Yields 4 servings.

Lemon Lentil Salad

½ cup dry lentils
2 cups water
½ cup long-grain rice
½ cup chopped red or green bell pepper
⅓ cup shredded carrot
¼ cup finely diced celery
¼ cup thinly sliced green onion
3 tablespoons olive oil
½ teaspoon finely shredded lemon peel
3 tablespoons fresh lemon juice
1½ teaspoons snipped fresh basil
¼ teaspoon salt
lettuce leaves
1 medium tomato, cut into 8 wedges
4 ounces cheddar cheese, sliced

- Rinse lentils. Check for small stones. Place in saucepan and add water. Bring to boil, cover and reduce heat.
- Simmer 5 minutes. Add uncooked rice. Cover.
- Simmer 15 minutes more. Remove from heat. Let stand, covered, for 10 minutes. Drain. Rinse with cold water and drain again.
- In large bowl, toss together lentil mixture, pepper, carrot, celery and onion. Set aside.
- In small bowl, whisk together oil, lemon peel, lemon juice, basil and salt. Pour over salad mixture and toss. Cover.
- Chill 2-24 hours.
- Serve spooned on lettuce. Garnish with tomato and cheese.

Yields 4 servings.

Chicken and Pear Salad with Tarragon

3 cups cubed, cooked
  chicken breast
2 cups chopped firm pears
½ cup sliced red onion
¾ cup chopped celery
¾ cup chopped mushrooms
½ cup chopped green onion
2 tablespoons chopped fresh
  tarragon leaves
  Lemon-Mayonnaise
  Dressing
  romaine lettuce or salad
  greens of choice

- Combine chicken with pears, red onion, celery, mushrooms, onion and tarragon. Toss gently. Pour lemon-mayonnaise dressing over mixture and toss again. Cover and refrigerate at least 1 hour.

- Serve on lettuce leaves.

Lemon-Mayonnaise Dressing

½ cup nonfat plain yogurt
2 tablespoons mayonnaise
2 teaspoons grated lemon
  peel
2 tablespoons lemon juice
1 tablespoon white wine
  vinegar
1 tablespoon Dijon mustard
½ teaspoon salt
¼ teaspoon pepper

- Combine all ingredients. Mix well.

Yields 6 servings.

Spinach and Sprouts with Sesame Dressing

Salad

½ **pound fresh spinach**
2 **cups fresh bean sprouts**
1 **8½-ounce can water chestnuts, drained and sliced**
¼ **cup toasted slivered almonds**
1 **cup croutons**
Sesame Dressing

- Tear spinach into bite-size pieces.
- Toss with bean sprouts, water chestnuts and almonds. Garnish with croutons. Toss with sesame dressing.

Sesame Dressing

¼ **cup soy sauce**
2 **tablespoons toasted sesame seeds**
2 **tablespoons fresh lemon juice**
1 **tablespoon finely chopped onion**
½ **teaspoon sugar**
¼ **teaspoon pepper**

- Shake all ingredients together in tightly-covered jar.

Yields 8 servings.

Variation: Substitute curly endive or romaine lettuce for spinach.

Italian Rotini Salad

Salad

2¼ cups Rotini pasta
1 cup cubed mozzarella or provolone cheese
6 ounces salami, sliced and cut into strips
1 cup thinly sliced cauliflower florets
1 cup thinly sliced zucchini
½ cup chopped red or yellow bell pepper
1 small red onion, thinly sliced and separated into rings
⅓ cup sliced, pitted ripe olives
¼ cup snipped fresh parsley
Dressing
3 small tomatoes, cut into wedges
2 tablespoons freshly grated Parmesan cheese

Dressing

⅓ cup olive oil
⅓ cup wine vinegar
2 cloves garlic, minced
2 teaspoons crushed dried basil
1 teaspoon crushed dried oregano
½ teaspoon sugar
½ teaspoon pepper

- Cook pasta al dente, according to package directions. Drain and rinse with cold water. Drain again.

- In large salad bowl, toss together rotini, cheese, salami, cauliflower, zucchini, pepper, onion, olives and parsley. Pour dressing over mixture and gently toss. Garnish with tomatoes and sprinkle with Parmesan cheese.

- In medium bowl, whisk together all dressing ingredients until blended and thickened.

Yields 10-12 servings.

Based on 12 servings:
251 calories; 14 grams fat; 50% calories from fat; 312 mg. sodium

Baked Curried Chicken Salad

2 cups cubed, cooked
  chicken breasts
¾ cup mayonnaise
2 tablespoons finely
  chopped onion
2 tablespoons capers,
  drained
1¼ teaspoons curry powder
¼ teaspoon salt
4 stalks celery, thinly sliced
½ cup toasted slivered
  almonds

- Preheat oven to 350°.
- Combine all ingredients except almonds. Pour into ungreased 1-quart casserole or six 1-cup baking dishes. Sprinkle with almonds.
- Bake uncovered 20 minutes. Serve.

Yields 6 servings.

Variation: Serve hot or cold as a salad or sandwich filling.

Greek Rice Salad

Salad

1 cup long-grain brown rice
1 cup frozen peas, thawed
½ cup feta cheese, cubed
½ pound tofu, cubed
  fresh dill, minced, to taste
½ cup chopped parsley
  leftover cooked vegetables
    such as carrots
  black olives
  Vinaigrette

- Cook rice in rapidly boiling water about 25 minutes or until al dente. Drain, rinse with cold water and drain again.
- Toss all ingredients with vinaigrette.
- Refrigerate 3 hours and serve.

Vinaigrette

½ cup olive oil
¼ cup lemon juice
  salt and pepper

- Blend all ingredients to taste.

Yields 6-8 servings.

Japanese Cucumbers in Sour Cream

1½ cups sour cream
1 small-medium Maui onion, sliced
⅓ cup lemon juice
½ teaspoon dill weed
¼ cup chopped parsley
1 teaspoon salt
dash of pepper
4-5 Japanese cucumbers, thinly sliced

- Combine sour cream, onion, lemon juice, dill, parsley, salt and pepper. Mix well.
- Add cucumbers and marinate several hours in refrigerator. Serve chilled.

Yields 8-10 servings.

Marinated Leek Salad

4 leeks, white part trimmed and sliced
1 tablespoon olive oil
Tomato Vinaigrette, divided
¼ cup dill sprigs, finely minced
2 tomatoes, peeled, seeded and diced
1 tablespoon capers
4 leaves butter lettuce
8 sprigs chicory
4 large sprigs dill

- Sauté leeks in oil until soft. Marinate in 2 tablespoons Tomato Vinaigrette for 1 hour.
- Place marinated leeks on chilled salad plates. Sprinkle with dill sprigs. Surround leeks with diced tomato and capers. Fan out lettuce, chicory and dill sprigs on plate.
- Drizzle remaining Tomato Vinaigrette to taste on salad before serving.

Tomato Vinaigrette

½ cup olive oil
2 tablespoons vinegar
½ teaspoon Dijon mustard
1 tomato, peeled and seeded
1 teaspoon sugar
salt and pepper, to taste

- Place all ingredients in blender or food processor and process until smooth.

Yields 4 servings.

Spinach Salad with Chutney Dressing

1 pound fresh spinach,
   trimmed and torn in
   bite-size pieces
6 fresh mushrooms, sliced
1 cup water chestnuts,
   sliced
6 slices bacon, fried and
   crumbled
½ cup shredded Gruyère
   cheese

- Combine spinach, mushrooms, water chestnuts, bacon and cheese. Pour dressing over salad, toss and serve.

Chutney Dressing

¼ cup wine vinegar
1 clove garlic, minced
2 tablespoons chutney
2 teaspoons sugar
2 tablespoons coarsely
   ground Dijon mustard
½ cup vegetable oil
   salt and freshly ground
   black pepper, to taste

- In blender, combine wine vinegar, garlic, chutney, sugar and mustard. Blend until smooth. Add oil and blend. Add salt and pepper to taste. Refrigerate.

- Bring dressing to room temperature before serving.

Yields 4 servings.

Thai Green Papaya Salad

Salad

3 green papayas
2 tomatoes
½ cup cilantro leaves, chopped
Dressing
red romaine lettuce
savoy cabbage

- Peel papayas. Scoop out seeds and slice into thin strips.
- Peel and seed tomatoes and finely slice.
- Combine papayas and tomatoes. Gently toss with dressing. Add cilantro. Serve with leaf of romaine and wedge of cabbage.

Dressing

½ cup peanut oil
½ cup rice vinegar
2 tablespoons chopped Maui onion
2 tablespoons sugar
1 teaspoon chili powder
½ teaspoon ground ginger
1 teaspoon salt
1 teaspoon chopped fresh red chili pepper

- Combine all ingredients in food processor and blend.

Yields 4 servings.

Cilantro Chicken Salad

3 boneless, skinless chicken
   breast halves
1 tablespoon hoisin sauce
1 tablespoon bean sauce
3 cloves garlic, minced
1 tablespoon soy sauce
2 teaspoons sugar
2 teaspoons sherry
10 won ton skins
   vegetable oil for frying
   mix of lettuce, watercress,
   won bok or other greens
5 green onions, cut into
   2-inch pieces, then
   sliced lengthwise
1 bunch cilantro leaves,
   chopped
½ cup roasted peanuts
   Dressing

- Wash and pat dry chicken breasts.
- Combine hoisin sauce, bean sauce, garlic, soy sauce, sugar and sherry. Add chicken.
- Marinate 2-3 hours or longer.
- Preheat broiler.
- Broil chicken 10-12 minutes, turning once. Cool. Cut into thin strips.
- Cut won ton skins into ¼-inch wide strips. Heat oil and fry strips until golden brown. Drain on paper towels and set aside.
- Shred salad greens. Toss salad greens, onions and cilantro together. Arrange sliced chicken on top. Garnish with peanuts and won ton strips.
- Drizzle with dressing and serve.

Dressing

2 tablespoons sesame oil
2 tablespoons vinegar
2 tablespoons sugar
2 tablespoons soy sauce
1 tablespoon hoisin sauce
2 tablespoons minced garlic
1 teaspoon dried chili flakes

- Whisk together oil and vinegar. Still whisking, add sugar, soy sauce, hoisin sauce, garlic and chili flakes.

Yields 4-6 servings.

Slaw with Cilantro Pecan Pesto Daniel

Slaw

3 tablespoons golden raisins

½ cup hot water

8 ounces red cabbage, shredded

2 tablespoons toasted pecans, roughly chopped

3 tablespoons red pepper strips, ⅛-inch thickness

6 tablespoons Cilantro Pecan Pesto

- Soak raisins in hot water. Allow to plump, then drain well. Cool.
- Combine cabbage, pecans, pepper and raisins. Mix well.
- Add Cilantro Pecan Pesto. Toss and serve.

Cilantro Pecan Pesto

1 tablespoon fresh lime juice

1 tablespoon mayonnaise

1 tablespoon lightly toasted pecans, chopped

1 tablespoon olive oil

1 tablespoon pineapple juice

1 dash Tabasco sauce

2 tablespoons cilantro, chopped

2 cloves garlic, chopped

- Combine all ingredients in food processor and blend to smooth consistency. Cover and refrigerate until ready to use.

Yields 6 servings.

Warm Scallop Salad

1 raw artichoke heart,
   thinly sliced
4 mushrooms, thinly sliced
1 stalk celery, thinly sliced
2 small tomatoes, peeled,
   seeded and diced
12 asparagus stalks, peeled
   and thinly sliced on
   diagonal
2 hearts of palm, finely diced
½ cup broccoli florets, finely
   diced
½ teaspoon salt
4 teaspoons fresh basil or
   other fresh herb,
   chopped
2 teaspoons fresh lemon
   juice
5 tablespoons olive oil,
   divided
2 sprigs fresh dill, minced
   freshly ground black
   pepper
12 sea scallops

- Combine raw vegetables with salt, herbs, lemon juice and 4 tablespoons oil, or to taste. Set aside to marinate.

- Wash and dry scallops. Lightly sauté in 1 tablespoon oil 2 minutes on each side.

- Arrange vegetables on salad plate and place hot scallops on top. Sprinkle with dill and pepper. Serve immediately.

Yields 4 servings.

239 calories; 18 grams fat; 64% calories from fat; 471 mg. sodium

Peanut and Pea Salad

2 16-ounce packages frozen
   peas, thawed
2 cups salted peanuts
¼ cup finely chopped Maui
   onion
2 tablespoons finely
   chopped bacon pieces,
   cooked crisp and drained
1 cup mayonnaise
½ cup milk
½ cup sour cream
1 package buttermilk-
   dressing mix (dry)

- Gently combine peas, peanuts, onion and bacon pieces.

- Stir together mayonnaise, milk, sour cream and buttermilk-dressing mix. Pour over pea mixture to desired creaminess and toss gently.

Yields 10 servings.

Crab Cakes and Greens with Sweet Red Pepper Sauce

2 teaspoons olive oil

2 tablespoons finely diced red onion

1 tablespoon finely diced red bell pepper

1 tablespoon finely diced yellow bell pepper

½ cup heavy cream

⅛ jalapeño pepper, seeded and minced

1 teaspoon chopped fresh chives

¼ teaspoon chopped fresh thyme leaves

1 teaspoon chopped fresh parsley

pinch cayenne pepper

1 large egg, lightly beaten

½ cup fine dry white bread crumbs

½ cup ground unsalted macadamia nuts

salt

10 ounces fresh cooked crabmeat

equal quantities of oil and butter for frying

mixed greens

Balsamic Vinaigrette

Red Bell Pepper Sauce

- Heat oil in fry pan. Sauté onion and peppers until onion is translucent. Transfer to mixing bowl and cool.

- In small saucepan, combine cream and jalapeño pepper and reduce to ¼ cup liquid. Cool.

- When jalapeño cream is cold, pour into bell pepper mixture. Stir in chives, thyme, parsley, cayenne, egg and ⅓ of bread crumbs and ⅓ of macadamia nuts. Salt to taste. Add crab. Mix thoroughly.

- Mix together remaining bread crumbs and nuts and pour onto medium plate.

- Shape crab mixture into 12 round cakes. Roll in crumb mixture to coat. Chill for at least 2 hours.

- Just before serving, melt butter and combine with oil to reach a depth of ¼-inch. Fry crab cakes for about 4 minutes on each side until golden brown. Drain on paper towels.

- Toss mixed greens with vinaigrette and place on individual salad plates. Top with 2-3 crab cakes. Spoon Red Bell Pepper Sauce over top.

(Continued)

(Crab Cakes and Greens with Sweet Red Pepper Sauce, continued)

Balsamic Vinaigrette

3 tablespoons olive oil
1 tablespoon balsamic
   vinegar
salt and pepper

- Whisk together all ingredients.

Red Bell Pepper Sauce

5 tablespoons unsalted
   butter, divided
½ Maui onion, diced
½ large red bell pepper,
   diced
2 cloves garlic, mashed
2 sprigs thyme, leaves only
½ cup white wine
1 cup heavy cream
salt and pepper
juice of ½ lemon

- Heat 3 tablespoons of butter in saucepan until foaming. Add onion, bell pepper, garlic and thyme. Sauté until onion is translucent.

- Deglaze pan with wine and reduce until thick, about 5 minutes.

- Add cream and bring to boil.

- Pour into food processor and purée until smooth.

- Add remaining 2 tablespoons of butter, salt and pepper to taste and lemon juice. Strain and keep warm.

Yields 6 servings.

Asian Pasta Salad with Salsa

Salsa

1 cup finely diced fresh
   tomato

1 bunch green onions,
   finely chopped

¼ cup soy sauce

3 tablespoons seasoned rice
   vinegar

¼ cup finely chopped
   cilantro

2 teaspoons ground fresh
   chili paste, or to taste

½ cup finely chopped Maui
   onion

   lemon or lime juice

¼ cup grated daikon

- One hour before serving, combine all ingredients. Refrigerate.

Pasta

¾ cup daikon

¾ cup carrot

1 cup soba noodles, cooked

½ cup julienned won bok

½ cup julienned zucchini

- Shred daikon and carrot lengthwise into long strings to resemble noodle shapes.
- Toss together pasta and vegetables in salad bowl. Add salsa and toss gently. Serve immediately.

Yields 6 servings.

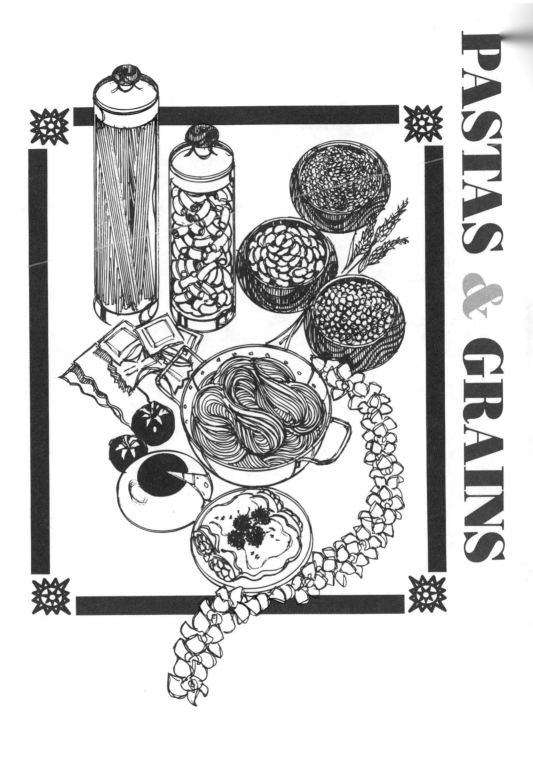

PASTAS & GRAINS

Pastas & Grains

Chilled Wild Rice and Vegetables

Healthy! Crunchy! Great for a hot day.

2 cups wild rice
2 tablespoons olive oil
4 cups chicken broth
½ cup vinaigrette dressing
¾ cup thinly sliced water
    chestnuts
½ cup thinly sliced red bell
    pepper
¼ cup minced green onion
    salt and pepper, to taste
¾ pound snow peas
½ pound mushrooms, sliced
2 tablespoons minced
    chives

- Rinse wild rice under cold water. Drain well. In flameproof casserole, heat olive oil over moderate heat. Add rice and cook, stirring often, about five minutes or until it starts to darken.

- Stir in chicken broth and bring to boil. Cover and reduce heat.

- Simmer 1-1½ hours until liquid is absorbed and rice "pops" open.

- Transfer rice to bowl. Toss warm rice with about ¼ cup dressing. Cool.

- In separate bowl, combine water chestnuts, bell pepper, onion, salt and pepper. Toss with half of remaining dressing. Chill at least an hour.

- Remove tips and strings from snow peas and blanch 30 seconds. Drain. Refresh under cold water. Pat dry. Cut on diagonal into 1-inch pieces.

- Toss snow peas and mushrooms in remaining dressing. Chill.

- Gently mix wild rice with vegetables. Sprinkle with chives and serve.

Yields 10 servings.

Tofu and Cheese-Stuffed Pasta Shells

Filling

¼ cup shredded carrot
2 tablespoons chopped green onion
1 8-ounce block of tofu
½ cup low-fat ricotta cheese
½ cup shredded cheddar cheese
¼ cup shredded mozzarella cheese
1 egg white, beaten
¼ teaspoon salt
¼ teaspoon pepper

- Simmer carrot and green onion in small amount of water until tender. Drain.
- Mash tofu. Stir in carrot-onion mixture, ricotta cheese, cheddar cheese, mozzarella cheese, egg white, salt and pepper. Set aside.

Sauce

1 16-ounce can tomatoes, cut up, undrained
1 3-ounce can tomato paste
1 teaspoon dried crushed basil
1 teaspoon dried crushed oregano
½ teaspoon sugar
¼ teaspoon garlic powder

- Combine tomatoes, tomato paste, basil, oregano, sugar and garlic powder. Boil, then reduce heat and simmer 10 minutes.

Shells

12 jumbo pasta shells
¼ cup mozzarella cheese

- Preheat oven to 350°.
- Cook and drain pasta shells. Rinse with cold water. Set aside.
- Stuff each cooked pasta shell with 1 rounded tablespoon of filling. Place shells in an ungreased 8x8x2-inch baking dish.

(Continued)

(Tofu and Cheese-Stuffed Pasta Shells, continued)

- Pour sauce over shells. Top with mozzarella cheese.
- Bake 25-30 minutes or until hot.

Yields 4 servings.

Pasta with Prosciutto and Gorgonzola

2 tablespoons butter
2 tablespoons olive oil
½ cup chopped prosciutto
4 shallots or green onions, chopped
2 tablespoons fresh thyme (1 teaspoon dried)
2 cups half-and-half cream
½ pound Gorgonzola cheese, crumbled
   freshly ground pepper, to taste
   crushed red chiles, to taste
¼ cup walnut pieces
1 pound ziti pasta, cooked al dente
½ cup Parmesan cheese

- Melt butter and oil in heavy skillet over medium heat. Add prosciutto and cook, stirring, 5 minutes. Add shallots and cook several minutes more.
- Stir in thyme. Add cream and Gorgonzola, stirring until cheese melts and sauce thickens slightly. Season with pepper and chiles. Add walnuts.
- Pour sauce over hot pasta and stir to coat. Sprinkle with Parmesan cheese.

Yields 6 servings.

Greek Rice Pilaf

1 large onion, diced
1 clove garlic, minced
¼ cup butter
2½ cups chicken stock
1½ cups rice
½ teaspoon salt
¼ teaspoon pepper
½ cup chopped fresh parsley
¼ cup brown or golden
    raisins
¼ cup pine nuts or sliced
    toasted almonds

- Sauté onion and garlic in butter until golden.

- Add stock. Bring to boil. Stir in rice. Add salt and pepper. Cover.

- Cook 20 minutes or until done.

- Add parsley, raisins and nuts. Stir and serve.

Yields 8 to 10 servings.

235 calories; 9 grams fat; 33% calories from fat; 522 mg. sodium

Korean Noodles

1 9-ounce package somen
    noodles
2 tablespoons soy sauce
1 tablespoon sugar
1 teaspoon sesame oil
2 tablespoons goma (sesame
    seeds)
1 chile pepper, chopped
1 2-egg omelet
½ cucumber, peeled and cut
    into thin strips
2 slices cooked ham, cut
    into thin strips
    watercress, roughly
    chopped

- Boil somen noodles according to package directions.

- Mix together soy sauce, sugar, oil, goma and chile pepper. Add sauce to noodles.

- Prepare very thin 2-egg omelet. Cut omelet into thin slices.

- Garnish noodles with omelet, cucumber, ham and watercress.

Yields 2 servings.

Spaghettini with Eggplant and Tomatoes

1 medium eggplant
½ teaspoon salt
1 tablespoon olive oil
1 small onion
1-2 cloves garlic
2-3 tablespoons mixture of
    fresh basil, marjoram,
    thyme and oregano,
    chopped
2½ cups canned tomatoes,
    undrained
2 tablespoons red wine
2 teaspoons paprika
    salt and pepper, to taste
1 16-ounce package
    spaghettini, cooked al
    dente
    freshly grated hard Italian
    cheese, to garnish

- Cut eggplant in cubes, sprinkle with salt and let sit 10 minutes. Rinse and drain.

- Heat oil in non-stick pan. Briefly sauté onion and garlic. Add eggplant and sprinkle with half of herbs. Cook eggplant until halfway cooked.

- Add tomatoes and stir. Add red wine, remaining herbs and paprika. Add salt and pepper, to taste. Simmer until eggplant is cooked and sauce has thickened. Adjust seasonings.

- Serve over spaghettini. Sprinkle with freshly grated cheese.

Yields 4 servings.

Variation: Add capers, olives, and sun-dried tomatoes (to cook's taste) while sauce is thickening.

Note: Soft eggplant can be bitter tasting. Choose brightly colored eggplants firm to the touch.

522 calories; 6 grams fat; 10% calories from fat; 525 mg. sodium

Pasta is cooked "al dente" when you take a bite and there is no white in the middle.

Linguine Puttanesca

2 tablespoons olive oil
4 cloves garlic, chopped
3 anchovy fillets, drained, coarsely chopped
½ teaspoon dried red pepper flakes
½ cup chopped onion
1 28-ounce can diced tomatoes, undrained
⅓ cup diced sun-dried tomatoes
½ teaspoon salt
12 Kalamata olives, pitted and chopped
2½ tablespoons drained capers
1 pound linguine
freshly grated Parmesan cheese for garnish

- In heavy skillet, heat olive oil. Add garlic, anchovies and pepper flakes. Mash with back of wooden spoon until ingredients form paste. Add onion, stir and cook until onion becomes soft. Add tomatoes, sun-dried tomatoes and salt. Cover.

- Simmer 15 minutes until sauce is thickened. Stir occasionally.

- Add olives and capers. Remove pan from heat.

- Cook linguine al dente. Drain well.

- Spoon sauce over individual servings of linguine. Serve with grated cheese.

Yields 4 servings.

Note: Sauce can be prepared ahead, covered and refrigerated.

Tortellini with Peas and Prosciutto

15 ounces cheese tortellini
1½ cups whipping cream
   freshly grated nutmeg
6 tablespoons freshly grated
   Parmesan cheese
1 cup frozen tiny peas,
   thawed and drained
1 ounce prosciutto, thinly
   sliced
   salt and freshly ground
   pepper

- Fill large pot with salted water and bring to boil. Cook tortellini until barely tender, stirring occasionally. Drain thoroughly.

- Bring cream to boil in heavy saucepan. Reduce heat. Add pinch of nutmeg and simmer until cream thickens slightly, about 8 minutes.

- Return tortellini to pot. Add cream mixture, Parmesan cheese, peas and prosciutto. Simmer over low heat until the tortellini are tender, about 4 minutes. Stir occasionally. Season with salt and pepper.

Yields 4 servings.

Somen Noodles and Sauce

3 quarts soup stock
12 inches dashi konbu
2 tablespoons salt
2 tablespoons sugar
¼ cup mirin
¼ cup soy sauce
1-2 8-ounce packages somen
   noodles, cooked
   green onions, thinly
   sliced
   kamaboko (fish cake),
   thinly sliced
   shiitake mushrooms,
   softened in hot water,
   stems removed and
   thinly sliced

- Boil stock, dashi konbu, salt, sugar, mirin and soy sauce together 30 minutes. Remove from heat and cool 10 minutes.

- Serve sauce with cooked somen noodles. Top with onion, kamaboko and mushrooms.

Yields 6-12 servings.

Pasta Primavera

1½ **pounds asparagus**
½ **pound mushrooms**
1 **carrot**
1 **zucchini**
3 **green onions**
½ **cup red bell pepper**
1 **cup broccoli florets**
4 **boneless, skinless chicken breast halves**
2 **tablespoons olive oil, divided**
1 **pound pasta, cook's choice**
2 **tablespoons butter**
2 **tablespoons flour**
¼ **teaspoon salt**
¼ **teaspoon pepper**
2 **cups milk**
1 **chicken bouillon cube**
¾ **cup Parmesan cheese, divided**

- Diagonally slice asparagus, mushrooms, carrot, zucchini, green onions, red pepper and broccoli.

- Sauté vegetables in 1 tablespoon oil until crisp-tender. Set aside.

- Cut chicken into cubes. Sauté in 1 tablespoon oil in nonstick pan until cooked through. Set aside.

- Cook pasta according to directions. Drain. Set aside and keep warm.

- Melt butter in saucepan. Stir in flour, salt and pepper. Gradually add milk. Add bouillon cube and cook, stirring constantly, until sauce is smooth and thick. Remove from heat and stir in ¼ cup Parmesan cheese.

- Pour pasta onto large serving platter. Spread sautéed vegetables over top. Add chicken pieces. Top with sauce. Serve with remaining Parmesan cheese.

Yields 6-8 servings.

528 calories; 18 grams fat; 26% calories from fat; 668 mg. sodium

Asian-Style Risotto

2 cups short grain rice
1 teaspoon grated fresh
   ginger root
1 teaspoon grated garlic
2 tablespoons finely
   chopped Maui onion
2 tablespoons vegetable oil
½ cup diced shiitake
   mushrooms
¼ cup finely diced carrot
2 tablespoons diced celery
2 tablespoons seeded,
   peeled and diced tomato
2 tablespoons diced water
   chestnuts
4 cups chicken stock
2 tablespoons soy sauce
1 cup diced, cooked chicken
2 tablespoons julienned
   fresh basil
2 tablespoons diced fresh
   asparagus
2 tablespoons grated
   Parmesan cheese

- Soak rice in cold water 1 hour, then drain.

- In large saucepan, sauté ginger, garlic and onion in oil until lightly browned.

- Quickly stir in mushrooms, carrot, celery, tomato, water chestnuts and rice.

- Pour chicken stock and soy sauce into mixture and bring to boil. Cover.

- Simmer 15-20 minutes or until rice is almost cooked.

- Five minutes before rice is done, add diced chicken, basil and asparagus. Add water if rice mixture is too dry.

- Cook 5 more minutes.

- Spoon rice into individual serving bowls and sprinkle with Parmesan cheese.

Yields 8 servings.

Gon Lo Mein

A popular Chinese noodle dish.

Stir-Fry Sauce

1 tablespoon soy sauce
½ teaspoon salt
2 tablespoons oyster sauce
2 teaspoons brown sugar
   (dark or light)
   dash pepper

- Combine all ingredients. Mix well. Set aside.

Noodles

1 12-ounce package chow
   mein noodles
1½ tablespoons oyster sauce
1 teaspoon sesame oil

- Preheat oven to 250°.
- Place noodles in 9x13-inch pan. Add oyster sauce and sesame oil. Mix until noodles are well coated.
- Heat 10 minutes.

Stir-Fry

1 tablespoon vegetable oil
1 small round onion, thinly
   sliced
1 9-ounce package chop
   suey mix or a
   combination of bean
   sprouts, sliced carrots
   and sliced celery
Stir-Fry sauce
Noodles, heated
2 green onions, cut into
   1-inch lengths
½ pound char siu, thinly
   sliced
2 tablespoons toasted
   sesame seeds
   cilantro to garnish

- In wok or large skillet heat oil and coat sides of pan.
- Place onion, chop suey and half of sauce in wok and stir-fry 2-3 minutes.
- Add heated noodles and green onions. Continue to stir-fry until vegetables are crisp-tender. Add remaining sauce. Do not overcook.
- Transfer noodles/vegetables to platter.
- Stir-fry char siu until heated. Sprinkle over noodles/vegetables. Sprinkle with sesame seeds. Garnish with cilantro.

Yields 6 servings.

Rigatoni with Chili-Garlic Oil

Pasta

7 ripe tomatoes, peeled, seeded and chopped

2 tablespoons Chili-Garlic Oil

salt, to taste

8 ounces Rigatoni, cooked al dente

1 tablespoon finely minced fresh parsley

1 tablespoon finely minced basil

freshly grated Parmesan cheese

- In saucepan, heat tomatoes with Chili-Garlic Oil. Add salt to taste. Keep warm over low heat while pasta cooks.

- Toss pasta with tomato mixture, parsley and basil. Sprinkle with cheese.

Chili-Garlic Oil

¼ cup olive oil

1½ teaspoons dried hot chile pepper flakes

1 clove garlic, slightly crushed

- Combine olive oil and chile flakes. Bring to boil. Cool. Add garlic clove. Marinate for at least 30 minutes. Strain. Chili-Garlic Oil will keep in refrigerator for a week.

Yields 4 servings.

316 calories; 8 grams fat; 23% calories from fat; 24 mg. sodium

Pasta with Shrimp Sauce

1 **pound spaghetti or cook's choice**

3 **tablespoons olive oil**

1 **small Maui onion, chopped**

1¼ **pounds shrimp, peeled and deveined**

⅓ **cup white wine**

1 **pound fresh ripe or canned plum tomatoes, peeled, chopped and drained**

salt and pepper, to taste

2 **tablespoons chopped parsley**

¼ **teaspoon red pepper flakes**

parsley for garnish

- In large pot, bring 5 quarts of water to boil. Add spaghetti. Cook al dente.

- While pasta is cooking, heat oil in large frying pan. Add onion and sauté until translucent.

- Add shrimp and cook 2 minutes on medium to high heat. Add wine and cook 2 minutes on high. Add tomatoes and seasonings and cook 2 more minutes.

- Drain pasta and place on platter. Pour sauce over top and garnish with parsley leaves. Serve immediately.

Yields 4-6 servings.

Seafood Pasta with Tomato-Basil Sauce

Tomato-Basil Sauce

4 Roma tomatoes, halved
¼ cup olive oil
¼ cup fresh basil leaves
 salt and pepper, to taste

- Preheat oven to 350°.

- In mixing bowl, toss tomatoes with oil and basil.

- Place in baking pan and roast 30 minutes or until tomatoes are soft. Place mixture in food processor and process mixture until coarsely chopped. Add salt and pepper.

Seafood Sauté

¼ cup olive oil
¼ pound bay scallops
¼ pound shrimp, peeled and deveined
2 tablespoons chopped shallots
1 tablespoon chopped garlic
½ cup sliced mushrooms
1 tablespoon chopped fresh basil
¼ teaspoon salt
¼ cup white wine
 Tomato-Basil Sauce
½ pound linguine, cooked al dente
2 tablespoons chopped parsley for garnish

- Heat oil in frying pan. Sauté scallops and shrimp until shrimp turns pink. Stir in shallots, garlic, mushrooms, basil, salt and white wine. Simmer 1 minute. Add Tomato-Basil Sauce and simmer 1 minute. Serve over hot pasta and garnish with parsley.

Yields 2 servings.

Rice and Fresh Mushroom Casserole

3 cups hot water
1 15-ounce can low sodium
    chicken broth, ⅓ cup
    chicken broth
1 cup wild rice, rinsed
2 bay leaves
2 cups white rice
2 teaspoons salt
4 tablespoons butter,
    divided
1 large onion, finely
    chopped
3 medium celery stalks,
    finely chopped
1 large clove garlic, minced
1¼ pounds mushrooms,
    coarsely chopped
    freshly ground pepper
    salt
1 cup chopped parsley

- Preheat oven to 350°.

- In medium saucepan, combine water, 15 ounces chicken broth, wild rice and bay leaves. Bring to boil over high heat. Cover. Reduce heat. Simmer 15 minutes over very low heat.

- Stir in white rice and salt. Cover. Simmer 30 minutes longer. Remove from heat and let stand uncovered until liquid is absorbed (about 10 minutes).

- Melt 2 tablespoons butter in large skillet. Add onion, celery and garlic. Cook over moderate heat, stirring, until onion softens and begins to turn brown. Transfer to large bowl.

- Add 1 tablespoon butter to skillet. Add fresh mushrooms. Cook about 8 minutes over moderately high heat, stirring occasionally until liquid evaporates.

- Add mushrooms and rice to onion mixture. Discard bay leaves. Season with salt and pepper. Toss.

- Place in baking dish and drizzle with ⅓ cup chicken broth. Dot with 1 tablespoon butter. Sprinkle with parsley. Cover with foil.

- Bake 30 minutes or until heated through.

Yields 4-6 servings.

Based on 6 servings:
441 calories; 9 grams fat; 18%
calories from fat; 1050 mg. sodium

Fettuccine al Salmone e Spinaci
(Fettuccine with Salmon and Spinach)

1 pound fettuccine

8 ounces cream

3½ ounces smoked salmon, cut into strips

3 tablespoons grated Parmesan cheese

7 ounces frozen chopped spinach, thawed

1 clove garlic, crushed

2 shallots, chopped, divided

2 tablespoons butter

7 ounces fresh salmon, cut into ½-inch cubes

7 tablespoons white wine

salt and pepper, to taste

- Cook fettuccine in salt water until al dente. Drain and keep warm.

- Pour cream in small bowl. Add smoked salmon and Parmesan. Set aside.

- Squeeze excess water from spinach and heat with garlic and 1 shallot. Set aside.

- Melt butter in fry pan. Sauté other shallot and add fresh salmon, white wine, salt and pepper. Simmer 2 minutes.

- Add spinach and smoked-salmon cream to pan. Mix well. Pour over fettuccine. Toss and serve.

Yields 4 servings.

One cup of tomato sauce equals a 13-ounce can of tomato paste plus ½ cup water.

Prawns and Pasta with Fresh Tomato Wine Sauce

2½ pounds tiger prawns, peeled and deveined

3 tablespoons olive oil, divided

2 tablespoons garlic, finely chopped

¼ cup finely chopped shallots

½ cup white wine juice of 2 lemons, strained

2 large tomatoes, peeled, seeded and chopped

10 basil leaves

¼ cup butter, cut into small pieces

salt and pepper

angel hair pasta, cooked al dente

- In bowl, toss prawns with 2 tablespoons oil to coat. Place on skewers. Set aside.

- Heat 7-inch sauté pan over medium heat. Add 1 tablespoon oil to coat bottom of pan. Add garlic and shallots. Sauté 5 seconds.

- Add white wine and lemon juice. Cook until liquid is reduced to ¼ of original amount, about 5 minutes.

- Turn heat up to high and add tomatoes. Sauté 30 seconds or until ¼ of juice has evaporated.

- Stack basil leaves and roll like a cigar, then cut into fine julienne. Stir butter into pan and add basil. Season to taste with salt and pepper.

- Preheat grill.

- Cook pasta according to package directions.

- Season prawns on both sides with salt and pepper. Grill (covered) for about 20 seconds per side.

- Place pasta on serving platter. Remove prawns from skewers and arrange on pasta. Spoon sauce over all.

Yields 8-12 servings.

Linguine with Macadamia Pesto Sauce

2 cloves garlic, peeled
1 teaspoon salt
2 cups tightly packed fresh
   basil leaves
2 tablespoons finely
   chopped macadamia
   nuts
½ cup olive oil
½ cup freshly grated
   Parmesan cheese
4 tablespoons butter,
   softened
1 pound linguine, cooked al
   dente
2 tablespoons reserved
   cooking water from pasta

- Combine garlic, salt, basil, macadamia nuts and olive oil in blender or food processor until smooth.

- Add cheese and butter and process just enough to combine all ingredients.

- Thin sauce with 2 or more tablespoons of hot water in which pasta was cooked. Process briefly.

- Put pesto into warm, large bowl, add pasta and toss well.

Yields 4-6 servings.

Walnut Asparagus Fettuccine

1 16-ounce package
   fettuccine
1½ pounds fresh asparagus,
   trimmed, cut into 1-inch
   lengths
1 tablespoon olive oil
¼ cup butter
1 cup half-and-half cream
½ cup freshly grated
   Parmesan cheese, extra
   cheese for garnish
½ cup coarsely chopped
   walnuts
   salt and pepper, to taste

- Bring water to boil in covered pot. Add pasta and cook al dente. Drain.

- While pasta cooks, place asparagus in wide skillet with water to cover. Bring to boil, reduce heat and simmer 4-5 minutes until crisp-tender. Do not overcook. Drain.

- Combine pasta with asparagus and add olive oil. Toss gently and return to pot to keep warm.

- In small saucepan, melt butter. Add cream. Heat until warm and slightly thickened. Do not boil. Add Parmesan cheese and walnuts.

- Pour cream mixture over pasta and asparagus. Add salt and pepper, to taste. Toss gently. Mixture will be slightly runny. Serve immediately. Provide additional freshly grated Parmesan cheese.

Yields 4-6 servings.

VEGETABLES

Vegetables

Broccoli and Sweet Red Peppers

Prepare this dish ahead when serving other dishes that require last-minute attention.

Sauce

- 2 teaspoons cornstarch
- 1 tablespoon sherry
- 1 teaspoon vegetable oil
- 2 teaspoons minced or grated ginger root
- 1 large clove garlic, peeled and minced
- 2 green onions (including the green tops), sliced crosswise
- 1 tablespoon oyster sauce
- 2 teaspoons soy sauce or 1 tablespoon reduced-sodium soy sauce
- ⅓ cup chicken broth

- Place cornstarch in small bowl and stir in sherry until mixture is smooth. Add oil, ginger root, garlic, onion, oyster sauce, soy sauce and broth, stirring ingredients to combine well. Set aside.

Vegetables

- 2 teaspoons vegetable or peanut oil
- 1 large clove garlic, minced
- ¼ cup sliced green onion (including green tops)
- 4 cups broccoli florets, steamed crisp-tender
- 1 cup julienned red bell peppers, cut into 1½-inch strips
- 2 cups carrot slices or sticks, steamed crisp-tender
- Sauce

- Heat oil in large nonstick skillet or in well-seasoned wok. Add garlic and green onion. Stir-fry 30 seconds. Add broccoli, red peppers and carrots. Stir-fry 1 minute.

- Stir sauce and add to vegetables. Bring to boil and cook vegetables, tossing continuously, 1 minute or less.

- Serve hot or at room temperature.

Yields 4-6 servings.

Colorful Vegetable Medley

4 teaspoons olive oil
1 pound zucchini, halved lengthwise and thinly sliced crosswise
2 large red bell peppers, cut into ½-inch dice
1 large green bell pepper, cut into ½-inch dice
1 cup snow peas, ends tipped, threads pulled
2 large carrots, peeled and thinly sliced on diagonal
2 cups thinly sliced red cabbage
4 teaspoons white wine vinegar
salt and freshly ground black pepper, to taste

- Heat oil in large nonstick skillet. Add zucchini, peppers, snow peas and carrots.
- Sauté vegetables 3-5 minutes, until crisp-tender.
- Add cabbage, vinegar, salt and pepper to taste.
- Sauté 3-5 minutes longer or until cabbage is crisp-tender. Do not overcook.

Yields 8 servings.

Note: Prepare in advance up to addition of last ingredients. Do final sautéing just before serving.

Hint: Vinegar brings out natural flavors without adding calories.

60 calories; 3 grams fat; 35% calories from fat; 13 mg. sodium

Carrots with Apricots

Apricots sweeten this carrot dish.

2 tablespoons butter
2 tablespoons water
1 pound carrots, shredded
10 dried California apricots, thinly sliced
1 tablespoon sugar
1 tablespoon red wine vinegar

- Heat butter and water over medium heat. Add carrots and apricots and sauté 2-3 minutes.
- Sprinkle sugar over top and add vinegar. Stir and cook rapidly 2 minutes until nicely glazed.

Yields 4-5 servings.

Sherried Carrot Coins

2 pounds carrots
4 tablespoons butter
1 small white onion,
    quartered
3 tablespoons water
½ teaspoon salt
3 tablespoons sugar
½ cup sherry

- Clean carrots and cut into coin-size rounds.

- Melt butter in pan. Add carrots, onion, water and salt. Cover and bring to boil over high heat. Reduce heat to medium-low. Cook 10 minutes until carrots are crisp-tender. Shake occasionally to prevent sticking without removing cover.

- Remove cover and discard onion pieces. Add sugar and sherry and bring to boil. Cover and reduce heat to medium-low.

- Simmer another 7-10 minutes until carrots are very tender and liquid is absorbed.

Yields 6-8 servings.

Christmas Beans

1 pound bacon
1 medium onion, diced
1 cup brown sugar
⅓ cup vinegar
½ cup water
1 can butter beans, drained
1 can green beans, drained
1 pink or white beans,
    drained
1 can kidney beans, drained
1 can pork and beans, pork
    pieces removed

- Preheat oven to 350°.

- Brown bacon. Set aside. Leave 1 tablespoon bacon fat in pan to sauté onion.

- Sauté onion. Add crumbled bacon, brown sugar, vinegar and water. Simmer 5 minutes.

- Mix beans in large casserole dish. Pour bacon mixture over all.

- Bake uncovered 1 hour.

Yields 4-6 servings.

Mushroom-Barley Skillet

6 tablespoons butter, divided
½ cup minced onion
1 cup barley
4 cups chicken or beef broth, heated
½ pound mushrooms, sliced
½ teaspoon salt
    pepper
    garlic salt, to taste
2 tablespoons snipped parsley

- Sauté onion in 3 tablespoons butter. Add barley and brown 3-5 minutes. Add broth. Cover.
- Cook 1 hour until barley is almost tender.
- Heat 3 tablespoons butter and sauté mushrooms. Season with salt, pepper and garlic salt. Mix mushrooms and barley together. Sprinkle parsley over top to garnish.

Yields 4-6 servings.

Herbed Oven-Fried Potatoes

2 pounds red potatoes, scrubbed and cut into 1-inch chunks
2 tablespoons olive oil
2 tablespoons minced fresh oregano or 2 teaspoons dried
2 tablespoons minced fresh basil or 2 teaspoons dried
1-2 cloves garlic, minced or pressed
8 tablespoons grated Parmesan cheese, divided
    salt, to taste
    oregano and basil sprigs

- Preheat oven to 475°.
- In large baking pan, toss potatoes with oil. Put in oven. As potatoes begin to brown, turn several times with wide spatula.
- Bake 35-45 minutes until potatoes are richly browned.
- Transfer potatoes to serving bowl and sprinkle with oregano, basil, garlic and 3 tablespoons of cheese. Stir to mix. Season to taste with salt. Top with remaining cheese. Garnish with oregano and basil sprigs.

Yields 6 servings.

299 calories; 11 grams fat; 32% calories from fat; 247 mg. sodium

Garlic and Rosemary Oven-Fried Potatoes

2 pounds small new
   potatoes, scrubbed clean
   and halved
1 tablespoon olive oil
3 cloves garlic, peeled and
   slivered
2 teaspoons fresh rosemary,
   crumbled
   salt and freshly ground
   pepper, to taste

- Preheat oven to 450°.
- Place potatoes in large roasting pan.
- Mix olive oil, garlic and rosemary. Pour over potatoes. Toss, coating evenly. Season with salt and pepper.
- Roast 25-35 minutes or until tender and nicely browned. Turn and baste once during baking.

Yields 6 servings.

Note: When tender, brown potatoes under broiler to speed process.

Roasted Potatoes with Lemon and Olive Oil

2 pounds new white
   potatoes or small red
   potatoes, scrubbed and
   quartered
¼ cup fresh lemon juice
1 tablespoon olive oil
   salt and freshly ground
   pepper, to taste

- Preheat oven to 450°.
- Arrange potatoes in large baking pan.
- Combine lemon juice and olive oil. Pour over potatoes. Toss, coating evenly. Season with salt and pepper.
- Roast 20-25 minutes or until tender and nicely browned. Turn and baste once during baking.
- When tender, potatoes can be browned further, if needed, by putting them under broiler.

Yields 6 servings.

Baked Sweet and Sour Red Onions

4 medium red onions
¼ cup red wine vinegar
2½ tablespoons firmly packed
    brown sugar
1 tablespoon olive oil
    salt

- Preheat oven to 350°.
- Cut unpeeled onions in half lengthwise, leaving root end attached.
- In large baking dish, mix vinegar, sugar and oil. Place onions, cut side down, in dish.
- Bake, uncovered, 30-40 minutes until tender when pierced.
- Serve at room temperature.

Yields 6-8 servings.

Variation: Make ahead and chill up to 1 day. Onions can be reheated 8-10 minutes on grill, turning often until slightly warm.

71 calories; 2 grams fat; 29% calories from fat; 5 mg. sodium

Buffet Beans and Cauliflower

This salad maintains its fresh color for hours. Prepare in advance and serve at room temperature.

1 **medium head cauliflower (1-1¼ pounds) broken into 1-inch florets**
¾ **pound green beans cut into 1-inch pieces**
1 **small red onion, thinly sliced**
Dressing
2-3 **tomatoes cut into wedges for garnish**
1 **bunch Italian parsley, chopped for garnish**
lemon wedges

- Cook cauliflower uncovered in boiling, salted water until just tender, about 3 minutes. Lift out florets with slotted spoon and cool under running water (or immerse in large bowl of ice water). Drain.

- Add green beans to boiling water and cook about 3 minutes. Remove beans and immerse in ice water. Drain.

- In bowl, combine cauliflower, beans and onion. Gently mix vegetables with dressing. Cover and chill 1-4 hours.

- Drain vegetables and place in serving bowl. Garnish with tomato wedges and fresh Italian parsley. Serve with lemon wedges.

Dressing

⅝ **cup olive oil**
⅜ **cup white wine vinegar**
½ **teaspoon dry mustard**
¾ **teaspoon sugar**
1 **teaspoon fresh basil**
1 **teaspoon salt**
¼ **teaspoon freshly ground pepper**

- Whisk together all dressing ingredients.

Yields 8-10 salad servings, 1 cup dressing.

Carrots with Raspberry Wreath

1 pound carrots, peeled and cut into ¼-inch slices

1½ teaspoons packed brown sugar, 2 tablespoons packed brown sugar

2 teaspoons salt, divided

1 10-ounce package frozen raspberries, thawed

1 tablespoon cornstarch

1 tablespoon Grand Marnier, raspberry or orange liqueur

¼ teaspoon freshly grated black pepper

finely grated zest of ½ lemon

- Boil carrots in water to cover with 1½ teaspoons brown sugar and 1½ teaspoons salt until fork-tender, about 10 minutes. Drain.

- Drain juice from thawed raspberries into medium saucepan. Stir in cornstarch and heat over medium heat, stirring constantly, until juice thickens. Stir in liqueur and gently fold in raspberries.

- When ready to serve, reheat carrots in microwave. Sprinkle with 2 tablespoons brown sugar, ½ teaspoon salt, pepper and lemon zest. Arrange carrots attractively on platter, leaving border around edge. Spoon raspberry sauce around border. Serve hot.

Yields 4 servings.

Simmered Kabocha (Pumpkin)

2 pounds kabocha

1 cup water

2 tablespoons soy sauce

2 tablespoons sake

2 tablespoons chopped, dried shrimp

2 tablespoons sugar

1½ teaspoons grated ginger root

½ teaspoon salt

1 tablespoon cooking oil

- Cut kabocha in half. Remove seeds. Cut into 2-inch pieces and peel skin at 1-inch intervals leaving strips of green.

- In large saucepan, combine remaining ingredients. Cover and bring to boil. Simmer 5 minutes. Add kabocha and cook uncovered, tossing kabocha occasionally, for 10 minutes until kabocha is tender and liquid has evaporated.

Yields 6 servings.

Summer Vegetable Kabobs

1½ pounds zucchini, cut into 1-inch rounds

1 yellow bell pepper, cut into 1-inch pieces

1 red bell pepper, cut into 1-inch pieces

⅓ cup olive oil

2 tablespoons red wine vinegar

1 clove garlic, minced

2 teaspoons chopped fresh thyme

½ teaspoon salt

¼ teaspoon pepper

8 large mushrooms, stems removed

8 cherry tomatoes

1 small Maui onion, cut into small wedges

- Fill saucepan with water and bring to boil.

- Blanch zucchini and peppers in boiling water 2 minutes. Drain and plunge into cold water for 2 minutes. Drain and dry with paper towels.

- Whisk together oil, vinegar, garlic, thyme, salt and pepper. Pour over blanched vegetables. Add mushrooms, cherry tomatoes and onion. Toss gently.

- Marinate 30 minutes, stirring occasionally.

- Preheat grill. Oil grill rack and place about 4 inches above fire.

- Using slotted spoon, remove vegetables from marinade. Save marinade.

- Alternate zucchini, peppers, mushrooms, tomatoes and onion wedges on skewers.

- Grill 8-10 minutes, turning occasionally and basting with marinade until lightly browned.

Yields 4 servings.

Variation: Make extra and serve cold vegetables in salad with chèvre and French bread the next day.

Guava-Glazed Yams and Bananas

This dish is wonderful with ham or pork chops.

2-3 cooked yams or sweet potatoes, peeled
4-5 small green-tipped bananas
2-3 tablespoons guava jelly
2 tablespoons butter

- Preheat oven to 400°. Butter 3-quart shallow casserole dish.

- Cut yams crosswise into ½-inch slices.

- Peel bananas. Cut lengthwise and crosswise into 4 sections.

- Attractively overlap yams on bottom of casserole dish. Arrange bananas around sides.

- Combine guava jelly and butter in small saucepan. Stir over low heat until melted. Spoon sauce over yams and bananas.

- Bake uncovered 20 minutes.

Yields 4 servings.

Party Potatoes

8 medium baking potatoes
10 ounces grated cheddar cheese
3 tablespoons milk
2 tablespoons butter
1 pint sour cream
1 bunch green onions, chopped
1 teaspoon salt
pepper, to taste
½ cup bread crumbs

- Boil potatoes, cool and peel. Grate or rice potatoes.

- Preheat oven to 350°. Coat 9x13-inch pan with nonstick cooking spray.

- Mix potatoes, cheese, milk, butter, sour cream, green onion, salt and pepper. Place in prepared pan.

- Brown bread crumbs. Sprinkle them over potato mixture.

- Bake 30-45 minutes.

Yields 6-8 servings.

Sweet Potato Orange Casserole

6 medium sweet potatoes,
    unpeeled
½ cup light brown sugar
½ cup fresh orange juice
1 tablespoon fresh lemon
    juice
¼ teaspoon salt
¼ cup butter

- Preheat oven to 350°.
- Boil sweet potatoes in covered saucepan until tender, about 25 minutes. Cool. Remove skin and cut into ½-inch cubes.
- Place potatoes in casserole. Sprinkle with sugar. Mix orange juice, lemon juice and salt. Pour over potatoes. Dot with butter.
- Bake 25 minutes.

Yields 6 servings.

Kartoffelroesti (Butter-Roasted Potatoes)

2 pounds large new potatoes
5 tablespoons butter
¼ teaspoon salt
    dash pepper
2 teaspoons water

- Cook potatoes 25-30 minutes in boiling salted water until just tender. Drain, cool, peel and finely dice.
- Melt butter in 10 or 11-inch frying pan. Add potatoes, salt and pepper. Stir to distribute butter evenly. Press potatoes into even layer in pan.
- Sprinkle with water, cover tightly and cook about 15 minutes over medium low heat until crusty and golden brown on bottom.
- Loosen potatoes with spatula and invert onto serving plate.

Yields 6 servings.

Eggplant with Shrimp and Crab

6 large eggplants
1¾ cups butter, divided
1½ cups chopped onion
1½ cups chopped celery
2 cups chopped green onion
7 cloves garlic, minced
1 cup chopped green bell
   pepper
1 cup chopped parsley
½ teaspoon poultry
   seasoning
½ teaspoon sage
½ teaspoon oregano
1 teaspoon garlic salt
2 teaspoons seasoned salt
1 teaspoon cayenne
2½ teaspoons garlic powder
2½ teaspoons onion powder
1½ teaspoons powdered
   chicken bouillon
2 cups medium shrimp,
   peeled and deveined
12 additional shrimp, for
   garnish
1 cup crabmeat
2½ cups unseasoned bread
   crumbs, divided

- Preheat oven to 350°. Lightly coat casserole dish or individual baking dishes with non-stick cooking spray.

- Place eggplants in large pot and cover with water. Boil over medium heat 30 minutes. Drain and set aside to cool. (Do not peel.)

- Melt 1 cup butter in large skillet. Add onion, celery, green onion, garlic, pepper and parsley. Sauté until tender. Add poultry seasoning, sage, oregano, garlic salt, seasoned salt, cayenne, garlic powder, onion powder and bouillon.

- Cook 10 minutes.

- Split cooled eggplants. Scoop out and mash flesh. Reserve shells for stuffing, if desired.

- Add mashed eggplant to the seasoned vegetables and cook for 10 minutes over low heat, stirring frequently. Add shrimp.

- Cook slowly 15 minutes.

- Add crabmeat and 1½ cups bread crumbs. Mix well.

- Pour mixture into casserole or individual dishes. If using eggplant shells, fill with mixture and place in individual ovenproof casserole dishes. (May be done ahead up to this point and refrigerated.)

(Continued)

(Eggplant with Shrimp and Crab, continued)

- When ready to serve, sprinkle with 1 cup bread crumbs, garnish with shrimp, melt remaining butter and drizzle over top.
- Bake 15-20 minutes. Place under broiler to brown slightly.

Yields 12 servings.

Potatoes with Mint and Sugar Snap Peas

½ **pound small purple or other boiling potatoes**
¼ **pound sugar snap peas, trimmed**
2 **teaspoons balsamic vinegar**
2 **teaspoons extra-virgin olive oil**
10 **fresh mint leaves, sliced in thin strips**
½ **teaspoon salt**
   pepper, to taste

- Place potatoes in heavy saucepan and cover with 1-inch salted water.
- Simmer 15-20 minutes or until tender.
- Drain (reserve cooking liquid) and cool 10 minutes.
- Bring reserved cooking liquid to boil and blanch sugar snap peas 1 minute until crisp-tender. Drain and refresh under cold water. Pat dry with paper towels.
- Quarter potatoes. Toss warm potatoes together with sugar snap peas, vinegar, oil, mint and salt. Add pepper to taste.

Yields 2 servings.

161 calories; 5 grams fat; 26% calories from fat; 591 mg. sodium

Spinach with Herbs

3 slices bacon
2 medium onions, thinly sliced
2 pounds washed spinach
½ cup coarsely chopped parsley
   1-inch tip fresh rosemary, leaves stemmed
1 teaspoon salt
¼ teaspoon pepper
2 tablespoons wine vinegar or lemon juice

- Cook bacon in large skillet until crisp. Remove with slotted spoon. Drain and crumble bacon. Pour off all but 1 tablespoon drippings. Add onions, spinach, parsley, rosemary, salt and pepper to skillet.

- Cook over medium heat until wilted, stirring once or twice.

- Add vinegar, sprinkle with crumbled bacon and serve.

Yields 6 servings.

Scalloped Potatoes

5-6 baking potatoes
4 tablespoons butter
1 large clove garlic, crushed
   salt, to taste
   pepper, to taste
½ pint heavy cream

- Preheat oven to 350°.

- Peel and slice potatoes. Place in bowl of water to prevent discoloring.

- Rub large baking dish with stick of butter to cover bottom thickly.

- Rub crushed garlic through butter in baking dish. Discard garlic.

- Dry potato slices and place in 3 rows in baking dish. Season to taste with salt and pepper. Dot with remaining butter. Pour cream over potatoes.

- Bake in oven for 40-50 minutes.

Yields 5 servings.

Entrées
Meats, Poultry & Seafood

Ginger Plus Pork Chops

4 loin pork chops, about 1-inch thick
½ teaspoon ground ginger
1 tablespoon unsalted butter
¾ cup ginger ale
¼ cup minced fresh ginger
¼ cup slivered, crystallized ginger
¼ cup chopped walnuts
¼ cup golden raisins
½ cup half and half

- Preheat oven to 350°.
- Sprinkle ground ginger over pork chops.
- Melt butter in large skillet and brown pork chops over medium high heat 2-3 minutes per side. Remove chops to flameproof baking dish. Retain drippings in pan.
- Add ginger ale, fresh ginger and crystallized ginger to reserved drippings.
- Cook 2-3 minutes over medium heat. Pour mixture over pork chops.
- Bake 15 minutes.
- Scatter walnuts and raisins over meat.
- Bake another 15 minutes or until done.
- Remove chops to serving platter and keep warm.
- Add half and half to baking pan. Cook over high heat, scraping up brown bits, until sauce is slightly thickened, about 2 minutes. Pour sauce over pork chops and serve.

Yields 4 servings.

Chinese Pork Steaks

¼ cup fresh lemon juice
¼ cup soy sauce
¼ cup honey
2 teaspoons Worcestershire sauce
½ teaspoon ground ginger
6 pork steaks or chops cut to ½-¾-inch thick

- Combine lemon juice, soy sauce, honey, Worcestershire sauce and ginger in a large, flat bowl. Place pork chops in mixture, cover, refrigerate and marinate 3-4 hours. Turn occasionally.

- Preheat grill.

- Place pork chops about 5 inches from coals.

- Grill 25-30 minutes or until done. Turn occasionally, basting with additional sauce.

Yields 3 servings.

Note: This dish can be baked in a shallow roasting pan in a 350° oven 45-60 minutes. Turn and baste occasionally during cooking.

Variation: Add ¼ cup mustard to marinade.

Baby Back Pork Ribs

5 pounds baby back pork ribs
½ cup soy sauce
½ cup ketchup
½ cup brown sugar
3 tablespoons honey
1 teaspoon grated ginger
1 teaspoon minced garlic
½ teaspoon salt
½ teaspoon pepper

- Parboil ribs over medium heat 20 minutes. Rinse in colander.

- Combine soy sauce, ketchup, brown sugar, honey, ginger, garlic, salt and pepper to make marinade.

- Marinate ribs 1 hour.

- Preheat broiler or grill.

- Broil or grill until browned.

Yields 6-8 servings.

Beef Broccoli

Beef

½ **pound top sirloin**
   Marinade
1 **tablespoon vegetable oil**
½ **inch piece ginger, crushed**
1 **clove garlic, crushed**
1 **pound broccoli florets,**
   broken into small pieces
½ **cup water or chicken**
   broth

Marinade

2 **tablespoons soy sauce**
1 **tablespoon cornstarch**
1 **tablespoon sake**
¼ **teaspoon salt**
1 **tablespoon sugar**
   dash of pepper

- Slice beef thinly. Marinate at least 10 minutes.

- Heat oil in wok or frying pan. Sauté ginger and garlic. Add beef slices and marinade. Stir-fry until medium rare.

- Add broccoli and water and bring to boil. Cook until cornstarch in marinade is blended and sauce thickens.

- Combine all ingredients.

Yields 2 servings.

Hint: Beef slices easily if slightly frozen.

348 calories; 14 grams fat; 34% calories from fat; 1323 mg. sodium

For thickening, 1 tablespoon cornstarch equals 2 tablespoons all-purpose flour.

Pork Loin Roll with Roasted Red Pepper Sauce

12 ounces pork tenderloin
1 cup loosely packed
   spinach leaves, stems
   removed
½ cup finely chopped fresh
   mushrooms
⅓ cup snipped fresh basil
2 tablespoons fine dry
   bread crumbs
1 tablespoon finely
   shredded Parmesan
   cheese
1 egg white, slightly beaten
1 teaspoon olive oil
   coarsely ground black
   pepper
   Roasted Red Pepper Sauce

- Preheat gas grill or start coals.

- Trim any fat from meat. Make lengthwise cut down center of tenderloin, cutting to, but not through, other side. Spread meat open. Place between 2 pieces of plastic wrap. Working from center to edges, pound lightly with flat side of meat mallet to form 11x7-inch rectangle. Fold in narrow ends to make it even.

- Layer spinach leaves on top of each other and slice crosswise into thin strips.

- Stir together spinach, mushrooms, basil, bread crumbs, Parmesan cheese and egg white in a medium bowl. Spread evenly over pork.

- Roll up pork jelly-roll style, beginning at short side. Tie with heavy string at 1½-inch intervals. Brush all surfaces with olive oil. Sprinkle with pepper.

- Place meat on grill over indirect heat. Cover.

- Grill 25-30 minutes or until meat thermometer reads 160°.

- To serve, remove strings from pork. Slice across and arrange pinwheel slices decoratively on platter. Serve with warm Roasted Red Pepper Sauce.

(Continued)

(Pork Loin Roll with Roasted Red Pepper Sauce, continued)

Roasted Red Pepper Sauce

2 red bell peppers, roasted,
  or half of 7-ounce jar
  roasted red bell peppers,
  drained
2 teaspoons olive oil
1 teaspoon red or white
  wine vinegar
1 small clove garlic
  dash salt

- Place roasted peppers, olive oil, wine vinegar, garlic and salt in food processor bowl. Blend until puréed. Transfer to small saucepan and cook over medium heat until heated through.

Yields 4 servings.

Pineapple-Ginger Lamb Chops

4 lamb leg sirloin chops,
  cut 1-inch thick
1½ tablespoons sugar
1 teaspoon cornstarch
½ cup unsweetened
  pineapple juice
2 tablespoons chopped
  green pepper
1 teaspoon soy sauce
¼ teaspoon ground ginger

- Preheat broiler.
- Trim fat from lamb chops and place on unheated rack of broiler pan.
- Broil 3 inches from heat 6 minutes. Turn and broil 4-6 minutes or until desired doneness.
- While chops are broiling, stir together sugar and cornstarch in a small saucepan. Add pineapple juice, green pepper, soy sauce and ginger. Cook, stirring until mixture has thickened and is bubbly. Cook, stirring 2 more minutes.
- Place lamb chops on serving platter and spoon sauce on top.

Yields 4 servings.

Apple and Raisin Pork Loaf

1 egg white
¼ cup quick-cooking rolled
     oats
3 tablespoons raisins
2 tablespoons minced onion
1 teaspoon mustard
¾ teaspoon salt
¼ teaspoon pepper
1 8½-ounce can applesauce,
     divided
1 pound lean ground pork
⅛ teaspoon ground
     cinnamon

- Preheat oven to 350°.
- Slightly beat egg white in medium mixing bowl. Add rolled oats, raisins, onion, mustard, salt, pepper and ¼ cup applesauce. Stir well. Add pork and mix well.
- Shape mixture into 6x4-inch loaf and place in 8x8-inch baking pan.
- Bake 55 minutes or until well done.
- Combine remaining applesauce and cinnamon in small saucepan. Heat through.
- Transfer loaf to serving platter. Slice and serve with heated sauce.

Yields 4 servings.

*237 calories; 7 grams fat; 26%
calories from fat; 528 mg. sodium*

Mustard-Coated Pork Tenderloin

1 pound pork tenderloin
2 cloves garlic
½ teaspoon salt
1 cup fresh bread crumbs
   (about 2 slices)
½ cup chopped fresh parsley
2 tablespoons olive oil
¼ teaspoon freshly ground
   black pepper
3 tablespoons Dijon
   mustard

- Preheat oven to 400°. Lightly oil rack (or spray with nonstick cooking spray). Set on baking sheet.

- Pat pork tenderloin dry with paper towel. Tuck under narrow end and fasten with toothpick.

- Chop garlic cloves. Sprinkle with salt and purée with knife blade held sideways. Transfer purée to bowl and add bread crumbs, parsley, oil and pepper. Mix thoroughly to distribute oil and garlic.

- On waxed paper, line half of bread crumbs in strip as long as pork tenderloin. Coat one side of tenderloin generously with mustard. Place tenderloin on crumbs so they adhere to mustard. Repeat process until whole tenderloin is coated with crumbs. Place tenderloin on rack.

- Roast 30-35 minutes or until center is barely pink and internal temperature is 160°.

- Let stand 5 minutes before slicing. Remove toothpick.

Yields 4 servings.

259 calories; 13 grams fat; 44% calories from fat; 708 mg. sodium

Pork Tenderloin with Raisin-Onion Sauce

Pork Tenderloin

3 **boneless pork tenderloins, about 1 pound each**
Marinade Rub
Raisin-Onion Sauce

- Rub marinade over tenderloins. Place in non-corroding container. Refrigerate.
- Marinate 9-24 hours.
- Preheat oven to 425°.
- Scrape marinade off meat. Dry with paper towels. Place in roasting pan. Cover.
- Bake 30 minutes or until internal temperature reaches 160°.
- Slice pork diagonally and arrange on serving platter. Top with sauce.

Marinade Rub

3 **teaspoons salt**
½ **teaspoon freshly ground pepper**
1 **teaspoon fresh thyme or sage**
½ **teaspoon ground bay leaf**
½ **teaspoon allspice**
1½ **cloves garlic, thinly sliced**

- Combine all ingredients.

Raisin-Onion Sauce

2 **tablespoons olive oil**
1½ **cups thinly sliced Maui onion**
¼ **cup flour**
3 **cups chicken broth**
1 **cup raisins**
¾ **cup port wine**

- Heat oil in pan. Add onion and cook over medium heat until onion is translucent.
- Sprinkle with flour and stir quickly to combine. Continue stirring and add chicken broth, raisins and wine.
- Reduce heat and cook, stirring occasionally, until mixture thickens, 8-10 minutes.

Yields 6-8 servings.

Quick Cassoulet

Vary this delicious casserole with ingredients on hand.

4 links Portuguese sausage
   or low-fat sausage, such
   as turkey kielbasa, or ¾
   cup cubed ham (½-inch
   cubes)
1 tablespoon olive or
   vegetable oil
1 medium onion, chopped
   salt, to taste
1 14.5-ounce can chicken
   broth
1 large potato, peeled and
   cut into ½-inch cubes
1 15-ounce can Great
   Northern beans, rinsed
   and drained
1 tablespoon dried summer
   savory, thyme or
   rosemary
¼ cup chopped fresh parsley
   freshly ground black
   pepper, to taste

- Heat large non-stick pan. Add sausage or ham and brown lightly. To lower fat content, remove meat from pan after browning and wipe out rendered fat with paper towel.

- Heat oil in cleaned pan and add onion, salting lightly.

- Cook 2-4 minutes until softened.

- Add meat, broth, potato, beans and herb. Bring to simmer.

- Simmer, uncovered, 30 minutes. Stir in parsley and pepper. Can be served immediately, but flavor improves overnight.

Yields 6 servings.

Variation: Substitute any canned beans.

Note: Cassoulet freezes well.

Osso Buco (Braised Veal Shanks)

A piquant Gremolata sauce makes this old classic special.

3 tablespoons butter

1½ cups finely chopped onions

½ cup finely chopped carrots

½ cup finely chopped celery

2 cloves garlic, finely chopped

6-7 pounds veal shank or shin, sawed - not chopped - into 8 pieces, each 2½ inches long and tied with string around the circumference

salt and freshly ground pepper

flour

4 tablespoons olive oil

1 cup dry white wine

¾ cup beef or chicken stock, fresh or canned

½ teaspoon dried basil

½ teaspoon dried thyme

3 cups canned whole tomatoes, drained and coarsely chopped

6 parsley sprigs

2 bay leaves

Gremolata

- Preheat oven to 350°.

- Melt butter in heavy shallow casserole or Dutch oven large enough to hold veal pieces upright snugly in 1 layer. Add onions, carrots, celery and garlic. Cook, stirring occasionally, 10-15 minutes, or until vegetables are lightly colored. Remove from heat.

- Sprinkle salt and pepper on veal pieces. Roll them in flour and shake off excess.

- In heavy 10- to 12-inch skillet, heat oil until haze forms over it. Add veal, 4-5 pieces at a time, and brown over moderately high heat, adding more oil if needed. Remove browned pieces and stand side by side on top of vegetables in casserole.

- Discard almost all fat from skillet, leaving just a film on bottom. Pour in wine and reduce over high heat to about ½ cup. Scrape any browned bits clinging to pan. Stir in stock, basil, thyme, tomatoes, parsley and bay leaves and bring to boil. Pour over veal. Liquid should come halfway up side of veal; if it does not, add more stock. Bring casserole with veal and vegetables to boil on top of stove. Cover tightly and place in lower third of oven.

(Continued)

(Osso Buco [Braised Veal Shanks], continued)

- Simmer gently, basting occasionally, about 1¼ hours.
- Test tenderness by piercing meat with tip of sharp knife. Remove bay leaves.
- Place veal pieces on heated platter and ladle sauce and vegetables from casserole around veal. Sprinkle top with Gremolata.

Gremolata

1 tablespoon grated lemon peel
1 teaspoon finely chopped garlic
3 tablespoons finely chopped parsley

- Mix all ingredients together.

Yields 6-8 servings.

Kalua Pig

Bananas sweeten this tender and juicy pork dish.

1 4-5 pound pork butt or pork shoulder
  liquid smoke or 1 teaspoon rock salt
4-5 bananas, whole, unpeeled
  ti leaves or aluminum foil

- Preheat oven to 325°.
- Rub meat with liquid smoke or rock salt. Place whole bananas, unpeeled, on top of meat. Wrap in ti leaves or foil.
- Bake until done, about 40 minutes per pound.
- Discard ti leaves and bananas. Carve pork and serve.

Yields 6 servings.

Grilled Leg of Lamb

1 6-7 pound leg of lamb, boned and butterflied
½ cup fresh lemon juice
½ cup dry vermouth
6 tablespoons extra virgin olive oil
3 teaspoons salt
1 teaspoon freshly ground pepper
4 teaspoons dried oregano
¾ teaspoon dried thyme
1 teaspoon dried rosemary
8 cloves garlic, minced

- Lay meat in large shallow pan or casserole. Slash thick portions of lamb to make it lie as flat as possible.

- Mix together lemon juice, vermouth, olive oil, salt, pepper, oregano, thyme, rosemary and garlic. Reserve ⅓ cup marinade. Pour over meat, coating both sides.

- Refrigerate overnight. Turn several times.

- Preheat grill.

- Grill over medium-hot coals about 20 minutes on each side. Baste with reserved marinade several times during grilling.

- Because butterflied leg of lamb has varying degrees of thickness, finished lamb will offer diners a range of rare to medium meat. Internal temperature should be 150° for rare, 160° for medium meat.

Yields 10 servings.

267 calories; 12 grams fat; 42% calories from fat; 261 mg. sodium

'Ono Roast Pork

4-5 pounds pork butt
1 clove garlic, minced
1 8-ounce can tomato sauce
1 cup soy sauce
1 cup sugar

- Trim excess fat from pork and brown in heavy pot.
- Add garlic, tomato sauce, soy sauce and sugar.
- Cook over low heat, turning every 20 minutes, for 1½ hours.
- Let pork cool for easier slicing.

Yields 12 servings.

Potato and Ham Pudding

A quick dinner made with ingredients likely to be on hand.

1 clove garlic
½ cup finely sliced onion
2 tablespoons olive oil
4 ounces Portuguese
   sausage, bacon or Black
   Forest ham, finely diced
4 ounces grated jack cheese
3 whole eggs
2 egg whites
3 tablespoons water
¾ pound russet potatoes,
   peeled, grated and
   squeezed dry
   salt and freshly ground
   black pepper
¼ cup chopped cilantro or
   parsley
1 tablespoon butter

- Preheat oven to 375°. Spray 2-quart baking dish with non-stick cooking spray. Rub with cut edge of garlic clove.
- Sauté onion in olive oil until translucent.
- In mixing bowl, combine onion, sausage, cheese, eggs, egg whites and water.
- Stir potatoes into egg mixture. Season with salt and pepper to taste. Add cilantro or parsley. Transfer to baking pan. Dot with butter if desired.
- Bake 40-45 minutes or until top is browned. Serve hot or warm.

Yields 4-6 servings.

Sandi's Short Ribs

Ribs

4 pounds short ribs
1 clove garlic
3 1-inch pieces of ginger
  Sauce

- Parboil short ribs with garlic and ginger 45 minutes. Let cool.
- Marinate short ribs in sauce overnight.
- Preheat grill.
- Grill until heated through.

Sauce

1 cup ketchup
1 cup soy sauce
1 cup sugar
3 tablespoons oyster sauce
1 teaspoon pepper
2 tablespoons
  Worcestershire sauce

- Combine ingredients and blend well.

Yields 4 servings.

Mexicali Pork with Rice

1 pound fresh pork, cut into thin strips
2 tablespoons vegetable oil
1 cup chopped onion
4 cloves garlic, mashed
1 6-ounce can tomato paste
1¼ cups water, divided
2 15-ounce cans pinto beans
2 teaspoons salt
½ teaspoon cumin
½ teaspoon dried oregano
1½ teaspoons chili powder
1 tablespoon cornstarch
6 cups hot cooked rice

- Brown pork strips in oil over medium heat. Add onion and garlic and sauté lightly. Stir in tomato paste and 1 cup water. Cover.
- Simmer about 30 minutes.
- Add beans, salt, cumin, oregano and chili powder.
- Mix cornstarch with ¼ cup water and add to mixture.
- Simmer 15 minutes longer. Serve over bed of fluffy rice.

Yields 6 servings.

Stuffed Tri-Color Peppers

1 pound mild Italian
   sausage
1 large onion, chopped
2 cloves garlic, minced
2 medium eggplants, cut
   into ½-inch cubes
1 large tomato, chopped
¼ pound mushrooms, sliced
1 teaspoon thyme leaves
1 teaspoon ground cumin
1 teaspoon crushed fennel
   seeds
8 large bell peppers, (mix of
   red, yellow and green)
½ cup chopped walnuts
1 egg
1 cup shredded mozzarella
   cheese, divided

- Preheat oven to 400°. Grease shallow 2-quart baking dish

- Remove sausage from casing and crumble meat into frying pan. Brown over medium heat.

- Stir in onion and garlic and sauté until onion is translucent.

- Add eggplant, tomato, mushrooms, thyme, cumin and fennel seeds. Cook, uncovered, 15 minutes or until liquid has evaporated and eggplant is tender. Remove from heat and cool slightly.

- Cut off tops of peppers and reserve. Remove seeds.

- Bring large pot of water to boil and drop peppers and tops into water. Boil, uncovered, 3 minutes. Drain and refresh in cold water bath. Drain again. Place peppers in baking dish.

- To eggplant mixture, add walnuts, egg and ½ cup of cheese. Mix gently. Spoon into peppers and replace pepper tops. Cover with foil.

- Bake, covered, 25 minutes. Uncover and discard pepper tops. Sprinkle with remaining cheese and bake 10 more minutes.

Yields 8 servings.

Pepper Pork Chops

2 medium potatoes, peeled
   and cubed
2 tablespoons olive oil
6 medium pork chops
2 green bell peppers, sliced
1 red bell pepper, sliced
3-4 pepperocini (vinegar
   peppers in jar), sliced
¼ cup vinegar from
   pepperocini jar
   salt and pepper, to taste
   pinch garlic salt

- Boil potatoes until slightly done. Drain. Set aside.
- Heat olive oil in heavy skillet and brown pork chops. Remove chops. Add bell peppers to skillet. Cook until slightly underdone. Return pork chops and add potatoes.
- Cook 10 minutes.
- Add pepperocini and vinegar to skillet mixture. Cover.
- Cook over medium heat 5-10 minutes. Season with salt, pepper and garlic salt, to taste.

Yields 3-6 servings.

Meatloaf Madness

2½ cups soda crackers,
   coarsely crushed
2 pounds lean ground beef
½ pound breakfast sausage
   patties, broken into
   small pieces
1 large egg
2 medium onions, chopped
1 medium green pepper,
   minced
⅓ cup Worcestershire sauce
1 teaspoon salt
½ teaspoon ground black
   pepper
1 cup ketchup, divided

- Preheat oven to 325°.
- In bowl, mix together crackers, ground beef, sausage, egg, onion, pepper, Worcestershire sauce, salt, pepper and ¾ cup ketchup. Mix thoroughly but lightly. Place in 13x9-inch baking dish and shape into a loaf. Cover with aluminum foil.
- Bake 45 minutes. Remove foil and spread ¼ cup ketchup on top.
- Bake uncovered 1 hour. Let stand 10 minutes before slicing.

Yields 10 servings.

Lamb Shanks

2 lamb shanks
salt and pepper
flour
vegetable oil for browning
2 cloves garlic
½ cup wine
1 small onion, sliced
2 carrots, sliced
2 medium potatoes, cubed

- Sprinkle salt, pepper and flour on lamb shanks.
- Heat oil in Dutch oven. Brown shanks in oil.
- Stick one clove garlic in each shank. Pour wine over meat.
- Cook slowly 1½ hours.
- Add vegetables and cook 30 minutes more.

Yields 2 servings.

Tostada Casserole

2½ cups corn chips, divided
1 pound ground beef
1 15-ounce can tomato
  sauce, divided
1 package taco seasoning
  mix
1 15-ounce can refried
  beans
½ cup shredded cheddar
  cheese
onion, diced
green bell pepper,
  chopped
avocado, sliced
sour cream
salsa

- Preheat oven to 375°. Line bottom of 2-quart casserole with 2 cups of corn chips; set aside.
- Brown ground beef in skillet; drain off fat. Add 1½ cups tomato sauce and taco seasoning. Mix well. Spoon mixture over corn chips in baking dish.
- Combine remaining tomato sauce and refried beans; spread over meat. Cover.
- Bake 25 minutes. Sprinkle with cheddar cheese and remaining ½ cup corn chips. Bake uncovered 5 more minutes.
- Garnish with onions, peppers, avocado, sour cream and salsa.

Yields 6-8 servings.

Roast Pork Loin with Garlic and Rosemary

2 tablespoons olive oil, little more for roasting pan

10 cloves garlic, peeled

3-4 sprigs fresh rosemary, leaves stripped from stems

2 teaspoons black peppercorns

salt

3¼ pounds boneless pork loin

1 cup water, divided

- Preheat oven to 400°. Lightly brush roasting pan with oil.

- Place 2 tablespoons oil, garlic, rosemary leaves, peppercorns and salt in food processor bowl. Process until finely chopped. Set aside.

- Trim excess fat and sinew from pork loin. Fold open loin and spread half the garlic mixture over meat. Fold flap of meat back over stuffing and reshape loin.

- Tie pork roll tightly at 1-inch intervals with string. Place pork in pan.

- Roast 20-25 minutes or until it starts to brown.

- Remove pan from oven and pour ½ cup water over pork. Turn meat over. Return to oven.

- Roast 45-60 minutes longer. Turn 2 or 3 times during roasting so it browns evenly. When pan becomes dry, add remaining ½ cup water.

- Remove pork loin to cutting board and cover. Let stand 10 minutes to reabsorb juices.

- Remove strings and cut loin into ⅜-inch thick slices. Serve warm with pan juices.

Yields 8 servings.

Pork Kabobs with Apricot-Orange Marinade

1 pound pork loin
1 cup apricot preserves
1 tablespoon frozen orange juice concentrate, defrosted
1 tablespoon butter, melted
salt and pepper, to taste

- Cut pork loin into 1-inch cubes.
- Combine preserves, orange juice and butter. Add pork. Toss.
- Marinate 3 hours.
- Preheat broiler.
- Thread pork onto skewers.
- Broil 4 inches from heat 10-12 minutes, turning frequently to avoid scorching. Salt and pepper to taste.

Yields 4 servings.

210 calories; 7 grams fat; 30% calories from fat; 74 mg. sodium

Buttermilk Marinade

4 cloves garlic, chopped
1 tablespoon fresh mint, chopped
2 teaspoons ground cumin
1 teaspoon paprika
½ teaspoon ground cardamom
pinch cayenne
⅔ cup buttermilk
2 tablespoons fresh lemon juice

- In food processor bowl, combine garlic, mint, cumin, paprika, cardamom and cayenne. Process until combined. Add buttermilk and lemon juice.
- Marinate cook's choice of meats or vegetables 1-8 hours, turning occasionally.

Yields 1 cup.

Marinated Flank Steak

Marinade

¼ **cup vegetable oil**
½ **cup soy sauce**
1 **tablespoon brown sugar**
1 **teaspoon ground ginger**
1 **teaspoon dry mustard**
3 **cloves garlic, minced**

- Combine all marinade ingredients.

2-3 pounds flank steak

- Pierce steak with sharp fork and coat meat with marinade.
- Marinate overnight or minimum of three hours. Turn periodically.
- Preheat grill or broiler.
- Grill to desired doneness. Best if served medium-rare to rare, sliced thinly across the grain.

Yields 6-8 servings.

Variation: Thin, bite-size slices can be skewered on toothpicks and served at room temperature as a pupu.

Grill your favorite vegetables along with the rest of dinner. Sprinkle the vegetables with rock salt and olive oil before cooking.

Flank Steak with Mustard and Caper Sauce

4 tablespoons butter, divided
1 tablespoon vegetable oil
1½ pounds flank steak
   Mustard and Caper Sauce

Mustard and Caper Sauce

2 tablespoons Dijon mustard
1½ tablespoons capers
3 tablespoons dry vermouth
1 shake Worcestershire sauce

- In 12-inch skillet, melt one tablespoon of butter with oil over moderate heat. Add meat and cook 6 minutes per side (or until desired doneness), turning once.

- Transfer to carving board and cover with foil.

- In same pan, over low heat, melt 3 tablespoons butter with pan drippings. With whisk, stir in mustard, capers, vermouth and Worcestershire sauce. Let mixture thicken slightly.

- Thinly slice meat and serve with sauce.

Yields 4 servings.

430 calories; 13 grams fat; 61% calories from fat; 538 mg. sodium

Sauerbraten with Raisin Gravy

Meat

3 pounds rump roast
Marinade
1 tablespoon butter
1 tablespoon vegetable oil
Sauce
slivered almonds
potato, pasta, potato
  dumplings and/or
  applesauce

- Place meat in glass or stainless steel bowl. Pour marinade over meat. Meat must be covered with liquid. If necessary add more water. Cover bowl.

- Refrigerate 3 days, turning meat several times.

- Preheat oven to 375°.

- Heat butter and oil in casserole with well-fitted lid. Remove meat from marinade and pat dry.

- Brown meat on all sides on stove top. Pour ⅓ marinade over meat and cover.

- Bake 2 hours. If liquid is cooked away, add water. Test meat for doneness.

- Remove meat from casserole and keep warm. Leave liquid in casserole to make sauce.

- Slice meat, arrange on platter and pour some sauce over it. Serve remaining sauce separately. Garnish with slivered almonds.

- Serve with potatoes, pasta, potato dumplings and/or applesauce.

(Continued)

(Sauerbraten with Raisin Gravy, continued)

Marinade

1 tablespoon whole
  peppercorns
5 whole cloves
5 bay leaves
2 large onions, peeled and
  sliced
2 cups wine vinegar
2 cups water
1 teaspoon salt

- Combine all ingredients.

Sauce

½ cup raisins soaked in hot
  water for few minutes
1 tablespoon molasses
2 tablespoons flour mixed in
  water
  salt, to taste
3 tablespoons heavy cream

- Drain raisins and add to liquid in casserole. Add molasses. Cook a few minutes.

- Thicken sauce with flour-water mixture. Salt to taste. Sauce should have sour/sweet taste.

- Add cream and keep hot but do not boil.

Yields 6 servings.

Grilled Pork with Arugula

8-10 pieces pork loin or pork
  chops, thinly sliced
  salt and pepper, to taste
¼-½ pound arugula
  extra-virgin olive oil
½ cup Parmesan cheese
2 lemons, sliced

- Sprinkle salt and pepper on meat. Sear meat on medium-high to high heat until pork is no longer pink.

- Arrange meat on platter. Cover with arugula, drizzle with olive oil and sprinkle with cheese. Serve with lemon slices.

Yields 6 servings.

Kalua Chicken

1 2-3 pound fryer chicken
4-6 ti leaves
  2 teaspoons liquid smoke
  2 tablespoons Hawaiian salt
  3 tablespoons oyster sauce

- Preheat oven to 325°.
- Wash and rinse ti leaves. Strip off bone (hard stem) from back of leaf.
- Line roasting pan, large enough to hold fryer, with heavy-duty aluminum foil. Cut foil long enough to completely cover chicken.
- Line foil with overlapping ti leaves.
- Place chicken on leaves. Rub cavity and outside of chicken with liquid smoke, Hawaiian salt and oyster sauce.
- Wrap chicken in ti leaves by tying leaf ends or carefully bringing up the leaves to cover the chicken.
- Seal tightly with foil.
- Bake 1½-2 hours.
- Remove from oven and let stand at least 10 minutes.
- Open and shred chicken meat. Bones will fall off and meat will be tender.
- Pour drippings into oil separator, then pour juices over meat.

Yields 4 servings.

Variation: If ti leaves are unavailable, place fryer on bed of fresh spinach, then wrap in foil.

Chicken Dijonnaise

12 chicken thighs
1 cup Dijon mustard
1 teaspoon salt
1 teaspoon black pepper
1 cup dry white wine, divided
¾ cup cream

- Preheat oven to 375°.
- Marinate chicken thighs in mustard, salt, pepper and ¼ cup wine for 2 to 3 hours.
- Place chicken in single layer in 13x9-inch baking pan. Add any remaining mustard marinade. Pour ¾ cup wine over chicken.
- Bake 55-65 minutes or until tender. Baste with pan juices every 15 minutes.
- When cooked, remove chicken to a hot platter.
- Remove excess fat from top of juices in baking pan. Heat juices on stove top over medium heat. Add cream and cook until just bubbling. Pour over chicken and serve.

Yields 6 servings.

Hoisin Marinade for Lamb, Beef or Chicken

6 tablespoons reduced-sodium soy sauce
¼ cup hoisin sauce or sweet bean paste
¼ cup rice wine or dry sherry
2 tablespoons sugar
2 tablespoons minced garlic (6 large cloves)
2 teaspoons (or to taste) crushed dried red chiles or red pepper flakes
1 tablespoon canola or olive oil
lamb, beef, or chicken for four people

- Combine ingredients in medium-sized bowl. Add lamb, beef or chicken. Toss to coat well. Cover and refrigerate.
- Marinate 4 hours or overnight.
- Grill or stir-fry meat.

Yields ¾ cup.

Chicken in Ginger-Lemon Grass Broth with Udon Noodles

3-4 pounds chicken pieces, skin removed

2 quarts water

1 2-inch piece ginger, cut crosswise into 8 slices

2 stalks lemon grass, ends trimmed, cut into 1-inch pieces

1 carrot, chopped; 2 carrots, halved lengthwise and sliced thinly on diagonal

1 yellow onion, coarsely chopped

½ daikon, peeled, halved lengthwise, sliced thinly on diagonal

¾ pound snow peas, ends trimmed, cut on diagonal in ½-inch pieces

3 green onions, sliced thinly on diagonal

salt and freshly ground pepper, to taste

Udon noodles, cooked according to package directions

- Combine chicken, water, ginger, lemon grass, chopped carrot and onion in large soup pot. Bring to boil, skimming off foam.

- Simmer gently, skimming as needed, until chicken falls off bones (50-60 minutes). Remove from heat.

- Let cool 1 hour. Skim fat.

- Strain broth into clean saucepan. Remove chicken meat from bones and tear into bite-size pieces. Return meat to broth.

- Over medium heat, bring broth to simmer. Add carrot and daikon slices.

- Simmer about 7 minutes or until tender. Add snow peas and green onions. Simmer 2 minutes longer. Season with salt and pepper. Add Udon noodles. Serve hot.

Yields 6-8 servings.

Chicken with Sausage, Apricots, Prunes and Apples

¼ cup olive oil

1 pound sweet Italian sausage, cut into ½-inch slices

4 whole boneless, skinless chicken breasts, cut into 8 pieces

7 tablespoons red wine vinegar, divided

¾ cup chicken broth

¾ cup dry white wine

1 bay leaf

1½ teaspoons dried thyme
salt and pepper, to taste

½ cup pitted prunes, halved

½ cup dried apricots, halved

10 cloves garlic, halved lengthwise

1½ tablespoons Dijon mustard

2 large green, tart apples, cored, peeled and cut into 1-inch cubes

1 tablespoon chopped fresh Italian parsley

- Preheat oven to 350°

- Heat oil in ovenproof casserole. Brown sausage over medium heat. Using slotted spoon, remove sausage and set aside.

- Brown chicken pieces and set aside. Pour off excess fat.

- Add 4 tablespoons vinegar to casserole. Boil over medium heat, scraping up brown pieces. Add broth, wine, bay leaf, thyme, salt and pepper. Cook 1 minute.

- Add prunes, apricots and garlic and cook 1 minute. Return sausage and chicken. Mix gently with sauce and cover casserole.

- Bake 40 minutes.

- Remove chicken, sausage, apricots and prunes. Add mustard and 3 tablespoons vinegar to casserole. Whisk well. Add apples and cook over medium-low heat 5 minutes or until tender. Spoon sauce over chicken and sausage. Sprinkle with parsley and serve.

Yields 4-8 servings.

Chicken Greek Style

1 chicken, cut into pieces
4 potatoes, peeled and
    quartered
¼ cup fresh lemon juice
2 tablespoons chopped fresh
    oregano
1 teaspoon salt
½ teaspoon pepper
2 tablespoons butter

- Preheat oven to 350°.
- Arrange chicken and potatoes in large ovenproof dish. Pour lemon juice over chicken and potatoes. Sprinkle oregano, salt and pepper over all. Dot with butter.
- Bake uncovered 1 hour until nicely browned. Baste occasionally.

Yields 4 servings.

Variation: Serve with tomato and cucumber salad for an easy Greek meal.

Rosemary Chicken with Garlic

½ pound boneless, skinless
    chicken breasts
1 tablespoon fresh rosemary
2 cloves garlic, finely
    chopped
2 tablespoons olive oil
    freshly ground black
    pepper

- Preheat grill.
- Wash and dry chicken breasts.
- Mix rosemary, garlic and oil together in small bowl. Season with pepper.
- Dip each chicken breast in herb mixture, coating well on both sides
- Grill chicken on both sides until well browned and cooked through, turning once or twice (about 10 minutes).

Yields 2 servings.

Note: Scrape roasted bits of garlic and herbs from grill pan and spoon over chicken for extra flavor.

Turkey Cutlets with Mango-Mustard Glaze

Fresh mango taste makes this a special dish.

¼ cup mango nectar (or
   2 tablespoons frozen
   orange juice
   concentrate)
2 teaspoons Dijon mustard
8 2-ounce turkey cutlets,
   silverskin removed or
   slashed
4 cloves garlic, crushed or
   halved
4 tablespoons butter
1 mango, diced

- Combine mango nectar and mustard. Stir well. Set aside.

- Rub garlic onto both sides of cutlets.

- Melt butter in nonstick pan. Over medium-high heat, cook cutlets 2 minutes on each side. Remove from pan. Set aside and keep warm.

- Add mango-mustard mixture to pan. Scrape browned bits for added flavor. Cook until thoroughly heated, stirring constantly. Add fresh mango chunks and heat through. Spoon over cutlets.

Yields 4 servings.

278 calories; 13 grams fat; 42% calories from fat; 232 mg. sodium

Mustard-Marinated Grilled Chicken

2-3 **pounds chicken pieces,
   skin on**
½ **cup dry white wine**
⅔ **cup vegetable oil or olive
   oil**
⅓ **cup wine vinegar**
2 **tablespoons finely
   chopped onion**
1 **teaspoon Italian herb
   seasoning or thyme
   leaves**
2 **cloves garlic, minced**
½ **teaspoon freshly ground
   pepper**
¼ **cup spicy brown mustard
   salt, to taste**

- Rinse chicken and pat dry.
- Combine wine, oil, vinegar, onion, herb seasoning, garlic, pepper, mustard and salt. Reserve ½ cup.
- Turn chicken in marinade to coat. Cover. Refrigerate at least 4 hours or overnight, turning occasionally.
- Preheat grill.
- Remove chicken from marinade. Discard marinade. Place chicken, skin side up on grill. Turn and baste frequently with reserved marinade until done. Season with salt and pepper.

Yields 4-6 servings.

Miso Chicken

2½ **pounds chicken thighs
   (10 pieces)**
   **vegetable oil to brown
   chicken**
4 **tablespoons miso**
2 **tablespoons sugar**
3 **tablespoons sake**
1 **teaspoon mirin**
2 **teaspoons soy sauce**
1 **teaspoon salt**

- Brown chicken in oil in large skillet.
- Combine miso, sugar, sake, mirin, soy sauce and salt. Pour over chicken. Cover pan.
- Simmer until chicken is done.

Yields 5-10 servings.

Vietnamese Lemon Grass Chicken

1 whole chicken breast or
  two large chicken thighs,
  boned
2-3 stalks lemon grass
3 cloves garlic, chopped
1 teaspoon curry powder
1 tablespoon fish sauce
1 teaspoon sugar
  black pepper
2 tablespoons vegetable oil
  chicken broth, if needed

- Cut chicken into bite-size pieces.
- Peel tough outside layers of lemon grass. Slice and mince finely.
- Combine lemon grass with garlic, curry powder, fish sauce, sugar and black pepper.
- Marinate chicken in mixture for 20 minutes. Discard marinade.
- Heat oil in wok or skillet. When hot, add chicken and sauté until light brown.
- Reduce heat and cook until done, adding chicken broth if more liquid is needed.

Yields 3 servings.

Fried Chicken, Japanese Style

Chicken

2 pounds boneless chicken
  thighs
  Marinade
  cornstarch or potato
  starch
  oil for frying

- Cut chicken in slightly larger than bite-size pieces.
- Marinate at least 30 minutes.
- Drain chicken and coat with cornstarch. Shake off excess.
- Deep fry a few pieces at a time. Drain on paper towels.

Marinade

½ cup soy sauce
¼ cup sake
2-3 cloves garlic, grated
1 inch ginger, grated

- Combine all ingredients.

4-6 servings.

Thai Cashew Chicken

1½ pounds boneless, skinless chicken, cut into bite-size pieces
2 tablespoons vegetable oil
1 large onion, chopped, or 10 green onions, cut into 1-inch lengths
½ cup thinly sliced carrots
1-2 cloves garlic, minced
2 teaspoons minced ginger root or ½ teaspoon ground ginger
1 cup snow peas
½ teaspoon ground red pepper
1 teaspoon ground coriander
2½ tablespoons soy sauce
2 tablespoons oyster sauce
½ cup water
2 tablespoons lemon juice
1 teaspoon ground cumin
1 cup unsalted, roasted cashews
    cooked rice

- In wok or large frying pan, sauté chicken 2-3 minutes in oil. Add onion, carrots, garlic and ginger root. Stir-fry until vegetables are crisp-tender and chicken is cooked through.

- Add snow peas, red pepper, coriander, soy sauce, oyster sauce, water, lemon juice and cumin. Cook 1 minute longer to blend flavors. Stir in cashews and mix well.

- Serve immediately with rice.

Yields 4 servings.

516 calories; 28 grams fat; 49% calories from fat; 1053 mg. sodium

Grilled Basil and Lemon Chicken

½ cup fresh lemon juice
¼ cup olive oil
½ cup honey
2 cloves garlic, chopped
½ cup fresh chopped basil
½ teaspoon pepper
4 whole chicken breasts

- Combine lemon juice, oil, honey, garlic, basil and pepper. Add chicken.

- Marinate for several hours in refrigerator.

- Preheat grill.

- Grill chicken until cooked through.

Yields 4-8 servings.

Eastern Chicken

This dish is great for a picnic lunch.

**4 cardamom pods or 1
  teaspoon coriander**
1 cup plain yogurt
1 tablespoon ground ginger
2 teaspoons Hawaiian salt
1 teaspoon sugar
½ teaspoon turmeric
½ teaspoon chili powder
¼ teaspoon cinnamon
**3½ pounds chicken
  drumsticks, about 15**

- Remove seeds from cardamom pods and finely grind seeds.

- In large bowl, combine ground cardamom, yogurt, ginger, salt, sugar, turmeric, chili powder and cinnamon. Mix well. Reserve ⅓ cup marinade. Add chicken to marinade in large bowl and turn to coat well. Cover bowl.

- Marinate chicken in refrigerator 4-24 hours.

- Preheat oven to 450°. Place oven rack in upper third of oven. Lightly oil broiler pan rack and line bottom of pan with foil.

- Place chicken on broiler rack in pan. Roast 20 minutes. Turn and baste chicken with reserved marinade.

- Roast chicken 15 minutes more until done and golden brown.

Yields 4-6 servings.

Note: Cardamom pods are available in Asian grocery stores or in the Asian section of your supermarket.

Bangkok Chicken

3 tablespoons dry sherry
2 tablespoons soy sauce
1 tablespoon fish sauce
1 tablespoon water
1 teaspoon cornstarch
¼ teaspoon crushed red
   pepper
12 ounces boneless, skinless
   chicken, cut into bite-
   size pieces
1 tablespoon peanut oil
1 teaspoon grated ginger
   root
2 cloves garlic, minced
1 cup sliced carrots
2 cups snow peas, tips and
   strings removed
4 green onions, cut into
   ½-inch pieces
⅓ cup dry roasted peanuts
   hot cooked rice

- Combine sherry, soy sauce, fish sauce, water, cornstarch and red pepper. Set aside.

- Pat chicken pieces dry.

- Preheat wok. Pour in peanut oil and heat.

- Add ginger root and garlic and stir-fry about 15 seconds. Add carrots and stir-fry about 2 minutes. Add snow peas and green onion and stir-fry another 2-3 minutes until vegetables are crisp-tender. With slotted spoon, remove vegetables from wok.

- If necessary, add more peanut oil to wok. Heat. Add chicken and stir-fry 3-4 minutes or until chicken is no longer pink. Push chicken to edges of wok and pour sauce in center of wok, stirring constantly. Cook and stir until thickened and bubbly. Return vegetables to wok. Quickly stir. Add peanuts and stir.

- Cook until heated through and serve immediately with rice.

Yields 2-3 servings.

Honey-Glazed Chicken and Vegetable Stir-Fry

12 ounces boneless, skinless chicken breast halves
2 tablespoons honey
2 tablespoons vinegar
2 tablespoons orange juice
1 tablespoon soy sauce
1 teaspoon cornstarch
2 tablespoons peanut oil
2-3 cups fresh vegetables of choice (thinly sliced carrots, onions, red pepper, snow peas, asparagus, mushrooms, etc.)
hot cooked rice

- Rinse and dry chicken. Cut into bite-size pieces. Set aside.

- Combine honey, vinegar, orange juice, soy sauce and cornstarch in small bowl. Set aside.

- Preheat wok. Pour in peanut oil and heat to medium-high.

- Stir-fry vegetables 3 minutes or until crisp-tender. With slotted spoon, remove vegetables from wok.

- If necessary, add more oil to wok. Add chicken and stir-fry 3-4 minutes or until chicken is browned. Push chicken to sides of wok. Add honey sauce, stirring, and cook until thickened and bubbly.

- Return cooked vegetables to wok. Stir all ingredients and cook until heated thoroughly. Serve immediately over rice.

Yields 4 servings.

One cup long grain white rice makes 3 cups cooked rice.

Filipino Adobo Chicken

8 **chicken thighs**
8 **chicken drumsticks**
1½ **cups distilled white
   vinegar**
4 **cloves garlic, crushed**
2 **bay leaves**
½ **tablespoon black
   peppercorns, crushed
   lightly**
1 **cup water**
¾ **cup soy sauce**
3 **tablespoons vegetable oil
   cooked rice**

- In large stew pot, combine chicken, vinegar, garlic, bay leaves, peppercorns and water. Bring to a boil. Simmer, covered, 20 minutes. Add soy sauce. Simmer, covered, another 20 minutes. Remove chicken to plate.

- Boil liquid about 10 minutes or until it is reduced to about 1 cup. Cool, remove bay leaves and skim fat.

- Heat oil in large skillet over high heat.

- Pat chicken dry. Sauté chicken 5 minutes or until well browned.

- Transfer chicken to rimmed serving plate. Reheat sauce and pour over chicken. Serve with rice.

Yields 4-8 servings.

Fennel Chicken with Ham and Almonds

This is a good dish for a buffet as it can be prepared ahead and is even better reheated.

2 **slices bacon, chopped**	• Sauté bacon, ham and onion in 2 tablespoons oil in large frying pan until onion is soft and lightly browned, about 4 minutes. Remove from pan and set aside.

2 **slices bacon, chopped**
1 **pound smoked ham, diced**
1 **large Maui onion, chopped**
7 **tablespoons olive oil, divided**
8-10 **boneless, skinless chicken thighs cut into bite-size pieces**
   salt and pepper
2 **cups chicken stock**
¼ **pound whole almonds**
2 **tablespoons flour**
1 **teaspoon fennel seeds, crushed**
¼ **teaspoon salt**
   freshly cooked pasta or rice

• Sauté bacon, ham and onion in 2 tablespoons oil in large frying pan until onion is soft and lightly browned, about 4 minutes. Remove from pan and set aside.

• Season chicken pieces with salt and pepper.

• Add 3 tablespoons oil to frying pan and sauté chicken pieces over medium heat until browned.

• While chicken is cooking, combine chicken stock and almonds in another pan and bring to boil. Turn down to simmer and hold.

• When chicken is done, remove to plate and blot with paper towels. Remove fat from pan, keeping brown bits in bottom. Add 2 tablespoons oil and 2 tablespoons flour. Mix well. Stir in fennel seeds. Cook until flour mixture is well browned.

• Add ham and onion mixture back to frying pan. Cook 1 minute. Add chicken thighs, hot chicken stock and almonds. Stir well.

• Simmer over low heat 10 minutes or until chicken is very tender and sauce is a deep brown. Salt, if necessary.

• Serve with pasta or rice.

Yields 8 servings.

Ginger Chicken Breasts

2 whole, boneless, skinless chicken breasts

2 tablespoons vegetable oil, divided

1 tablespoon grated ginger root

1 cup bias-sliced carrots

3½ cups sliced bok choy

1 cup snow peas

3 green onions, sliced diagonally into 1-inch pieces

¼ cup pineapple juice

2 tablespoons low-sodium soy sauce

1 tablespoon water

1 teaspoon cornstarch

2 cups leftover cooked rice

¼ cup chicken broth

- Rinse chicken and pat dry. Cut into thin, bite-size pieces.
- In medium skillet or wok, heat 1 tablespoon oil. Add ginger root, carrots, bok choy, snow peas and onion. (Add remaining oil if needed during cooking.) Stir-fry until crisp-tender. With slotted spoon, remove vegetables from skillet. Set aside.
- Add chicken to skillet and sauté until no longer pink.
- Push chicken up side of wok or to edge of skillet.
- In small bowl, stir together pineapple juice, soy sauce, water and cornstarch. Add to center of skillet and cook, stirring, until thickened and bubbly. Return vegetables to skillet and stir. Add leftover rice and broth and combine until well coated and hot.

Yields 3 servings.

Chicken Zucchini Lasagna

Sliced zucchini replaces the pasta in this lighter dish.

- **2 tablespoons olive oil**
- **2 cloves garlic, minced**
- **1 large onion, chopped**
- **¼ pound mushrooms, sliced**
- **1 pound lean ground chicken or turkey**
- **1 16-ounce can tomatoes, undrained**
- **1 6-ounce can tomato paste**
- **¾ cup dry red wine or beef broth**
- **1½ teaspoons oregano leaves**
- **½ teaspoon dried basil**
- **salt and pepper, to taste**
- **6 medium zucchini, cut into ⅛-inch-thick slices**
- **½ pound mozzarella cheese, thinly sliced**
- **1 cup ricotta cheese**
- **½ cup grated Parmesan cheese**

- Preheat oven to 350°. Grease shallow 3-quart casserole.
- Heat oil in wide frying pan over medium heat. Add garlic and onion. Cook, stirring, until onion is soft. Add mushrooms and chicken or turkey. Cook, stirring, until meat is lightly browned, about 5 minutes.
- Stir in tomatoes, breaking up with a spoon. Add tomato paste, wine or broth, oregano, basil, salt and pepper. Simmer, uncovered, until thick (about 25 minutes).
- Arrange half the zucchini slices in prepared dish. Top evenly with half the mozzarella, half the ricotta and half the sauce. Repeat layers. Sprinkle with Parmesan cheese.
- Bake, uncovered, 35 minutes or until zucchini is tender when pierced and cheese is lightly browned.

Yields 6-8 servings.

450 calories; 21 grams fat; 40% calories from fat; 586 mg. sodium

Lime Chicken

2-2½ pounds skinless chicken
    pieces
  ½ teaspoon finely shredded
    lime peel
  ¼ cup lime juice
  1 tablespoon vegetable oil
  2 cloves garlic, minced
  1 teaspoon dried thyme or
    basil, crushed
½-1 teaspoon cracked black
    pepper
  ¼ teaspoon salt
1½ tablespoons soy sauce
    steamed rice

- Preheat broiler.
- Rinse chicken and pat dry. Place chicken pieces, bone sides up, on rack of broiler pan. Broil 4 to 5 inches away from heat about 20 minutes or until lightly browned.
- Stir together lime peel, lime juice, oil, garlic, thyme or basil, pepper, salt and soy sauce. Brush chicken with glaze. Turn chicken; brush with more glaze.
- Broil an additional 5-15 minutes or until chicken is tender and no longer pink, brushing often with glaze during last 5 minutes of cooking.
- Serve with steamed rice.

Yields 6 servings.

Chicken Jakarta

  ¾ cup chicken broth
  ⅓ cup smooth peanut butter
  2 teaspoons honey
  1 tablespoon soy sauce
  ¼ teaspoon crushed red
    pepper flakes
  2 tablespoons fresh lemon
    juice
  2 teaspoons peanut oil
  1 pound boneless, skinless
    chicken breasts, very
    thinly sliced
  5 green onions, thinly
    sliced, divided
    steamed rice

- Combine broth, peanut butter, honey, soy sauce, red pepper flakes and lemon juice. Set aside.
- Heat oil in heavy skillet over medium-high heat. Add chicken and sauté 2-3 minutes until cooked through.
- Remove chicken from pan, add sauce and 3 green onions. Boil until slightly thickened. Add chicken, stirring to coat.
- Serve over rice, garnished with remaining green onions.

Yields 4 servings.

Savory Oregano Chicken

1½ **pounds meaty chicken**
    pieces, skinned
½ **teaspoon salt**
¼ **teaspoon pepper**
1 **clove garlic, minced**
1 **lemon, thinly sliced,**
    divided
2 **large tomatoes, peeled**
    and chopped, divided
½ **cup pitted ripe olives**
¼ **cup chopped onion**
¼ **cup snipped fresh parsley**
1 **tablespoon snipped fresh**
    oregano or 1 teaspoon
    dried oregano, crushed
⅛ **teaspoon ground red**
    pepper
¼ **cup dry white wine**
¾ **cup chicken broth**
1 **medium green bell**
    pepper, cut into strips
1 **medium red bell pepper,**
    cut into strips
    fresh oregano sprigs

- Rinse chicken and pat dry. Sprinkle with salt and pepper. Lightly coat non-stick skillet with non-stick cooking spray.

- Cook chicken over medium heat 15 minutes until lightly browned, turning once. Reduce heat.

- Place garlic, half of lemon slices, half of chopped tomatoes, olives, onion, parsley and oregano over chicken pieces. Sprinkle with ground red pepper. Add wine and broth. Cover.

- Simmer 15 minutes.

- Add remaining tomatoes and bell peppers.

- Cook, covered, 5-10 minutes until peppers are crisp-tender and chicken is tender and no longer pink. Transfer chicken and vegetables to a platter.

- Garnish with remaining lemon slices and fresh oregano sprigs.

Yields 4 servings.

212 calories; 6 grams fat; 23% calories from fat; 697 mg. sodium

Chicken Kabobs

1 8-ounce can pineapple chunks

¼ cup bottled chili sauce

1 tablespoon brown sugar

1 tablespoon lime juice

¼ teaspoon salt

¼ teaspoon ground ginger

¼ teaspoon ground allspice

¼ teaspoon ground red pepper

4 boneless, skinless chicken breast halves

8 button mushrooms

1 Maui onion, cut into 8 chunks

1 large red or green bell pepper, cut into 1-inch pieces

- Preheat broiler.

- Drain pineapple, reserving 2 tablespoons juice; set chunks aside.

- Combine reserved pineapple juice, chili sauce, brown sugar, lime juice, salt, ginger, allspice and red pepper; set aside.

- Rinse chicken; pat dry. Cut chicken breasts lengthwise into 1-inch-wide strips. On 8 long metal or bamboo skewers, alternately thread chicken strips, accordion-style, with mushrooms, onion, sweet pepper and pineapple chunks. Leave about ¼-inch space between food pieces. Place skewers on rack of broiler pan; brush with sauce.

- Broil 4-5 inches from heat 5 minutes. Turn once; brush with sauce.

- Broil additional 3-5 minutes until chicken is tender and no longer pink.

Yields 4 servings.

Note: If using bamboo skewers, soak them in water 30 minutes before using so they will not burn.

Chicken Curry for a Crowd

5 pounds boneless, skinless chicken breasts (8 cups cubed cooked chicken)
½ cup water
½ cup white wine
½ cup butter
2 cups chopped onion
4 cloves garlic, chopped
1 cup chopped green bell pepper
1 cup chopped celery
4 tablespoons curry powder
2 teaspoons salt
1 cup flour
4 cups chicken broth, heated
4 cups coconut milk, heated
cooked white rice

Curry Condiments, Cook's Choice (see note)

• **hard-cooked eggs, chopped**
• **cooked bacon, chopped**
• **green onion, chopped**
• **sweet pickles, chopped or sliced**
• **shredded coconut**
• **macadamia nuts, chopped**
• **sweet melon rind or kumquats**
• **chutney**
• **raisins**
• **tomatoes, chopped**

• Poach chicken pieces in water and white wine until tender. Cool. Cube.

• Melt butter in large saucepan. Add onion, garlic, pepper and celery. Cook until onion is translucent.

• Add curry powder, salt and flour. Mix well and cook over low heat for 2 minutes to cook flour. Remove from heat.

• Gradually add chicken broth and coconut milk. Heat to boiling. Lower heat and cook 3 minutes, stirring constantly.

• Add chicken. Heat, stirring occasionally, 10 minutes.

• Serve over rice with any condiments.

Yields 20-24 servings.

Hint: Recipe can be doubled or tripled.

Note: The number of condiments offered must be an odd number unless there are 10. Ten is a lucky number in some Asian cultures and 10 condiments are permissible.

Hard boiled eggs are easier to peel if they are cooked after they are a few days old.

Chicken Enchiladas

This is a low-calorie yet full-flavored version.

½ pound boneless, skinless chicken breasts

4 cups torn fresh spinach (or ½ of 10-ounce package of frozen chopped spinach, thawed and well-drained)

3 green onions, thinly sliced

1 8-ounce carton light sour cream

⅓ cup plain fat-free yogurt

2 tablespoons flour

¼ teaspoon ground cumin

¼ teaspoon salt

½ cup skim milk

1 4-ounce can diced green chile peppers, drained

6 7-inch flour tortillas

⅓ cup shredded, reduced fat cheddar or Monterey Jack cheese

chopped tomato or salsa

thinly sliced green onion

- Place chicken in saucepan and cover with water. Bring to boil, reduce heat. Cover.

- Simmer 15 minutes or until chicken is cooked through. Remove chicken from pan and cool. Shred chicken with fork into bite-size pieces. Set aside.

- Preheat oven to 350°.

- Place fresh spinach in steamer basket over boiling water. Reduce heat and steam, covered, 3-5 minutes. Or place in pan with small amount of boiling water, cover and cook 3-5 minutes. Drain well. Squeeze out extra moisture.

- Combine chicken, spinach and green onion in large bowl. Set aside.

- Combine sour cream, yogurt, flour, cumin and salt. Add milk and chile peppers. Stir well.

- Combine half of sauce with chicken-spinach mixture.

- Place ⅙ of filling mixture on each tortilla. Roll and place seam side down in ungreased, rectangular baking dish. Repeat with all tortillas.

- Spoon remaining sauce over filled tortillas. Bake, uncovered, about 25 minutes or until heated through. Sprinkle with cheese. Let stand 5 minutes. Transfer to serving platter.

(Continued)

(Chicken Enchiladas, continued)

- Garnish with chopped tomato or salsa and green onion.

Yields 6 servings.

Note: After filling and rolling tortillas, dish can be covered and refrigerated up to 24 hours. Refrigerate reserved sauce in separate, covered container. Add 10-15 minutes baking time.

297 calories; 8 grams fat; 24% calories from fat; 528 mg. sodium

Herb-Roasted Chicken

1 whole, broiler-fryer chicken
2 tablespoons butter, melted
2 cloves garlic, minced
1 teaspoon dried basil, crushed
½ teaspoon tarragon
½ teaspoon salt
½ teaspoon ground sage
½ teaspoon dried thyme, crushed
¼ teaspoon lemon-pepper seasoning or pepper

- Preheat oven to 375°.

- Rinse chicken. Pat dry. Truss chicken for baking. Place chicken, breast side up, on rack in shallow roasting pan. Brush with melted butter.

- Combine garlic, basil, tarragon, salt, sage, thyme, and lemon-pepper seasoning. Rub onto chicken. Insert meat thermometer into center of thigh muscle.

- Roast uncovered 1-1¼ hours until skin is nicely browned, drumsticks move easily in their sockets and meat thermometer registers 180°-185°. Remove chicken from oven. Let stand 10 minutes before carving.

Yields 6 servings.

Emilia-Romagna Chicken

1½ pounds boneless, skinless
    chicken breasts, cut into
    bite-size pieces
    freshly ground black
    pepper
    flour for dredging
¼ pound bacon
1 cup sliced mushrooms
1 tablespoon olive oil
3 cloves garlic, minced
1 cup chicken broth
½ cup red wine
½ cup balsamic vinegar
1 teaspoon arrowroot,
    dissolved in 2
    tablespoons cold water
¼ cup canned tomatoes,
    drained
    chopped parsley
    cooked rice

- Season chicken with pepper. Dip in flour and shake off excess.

- In non-stick pan, cook bacon until crisp. Remove from pan, drain on paper towels and dice. Pour bacon drippings from pan. Set aside.

- Return 2 tablespoons bacon drippings to pan. Add chicken and brown 10 minutes. Transfer to plate.

- Brown mushrooms in same pan 10 minutes. If necessary, add a little more bacon drippings. Set aside.

- In clean sauté pan, heat oil. Add garlic and sauté briefly. Pour in broth, wine and balsamic vinegar and boil 4 minutes. Pour in arrowroot mixture and stir. Add tomatoes and chicken.

- Simmer 10-15 minutes.

- Stir in mushrooms.

- Transfer to heated serving plate and garnish with parsley and chopped bacon. Serve with rice.

Yields 4-6 servings.

Zesty Beer Chicken with Onions

6 boneless, skinless chicken breast halves

⅓ cup flour

½ teaspoon salt

½ teaspoon pepper

3 tablespoons butter

3 tablespoons vegetable oil

2 Maui onions, sliced

1 12-ounce bottle beer

1 cup chili sauce

- Preheat oven to 325°.
- Rinse chicken and pat dry.
- Combine flour, salt and pepper. Dredge each chicken piece in mixture.
- In large fry pan, heat butter and oil. Add chicken pieces and 1 sliced onion. Brown chicken and onion on all sides. Place chicken and onion in large baking pan.
- Mix together beer and chili sauce and pour over chicken. Arrange remaining sliced onion on top.
- Bake, uncovered, 45 minutes or until tender.

Note: Serve with steamed rice or baked beans.

Yields 6 servings.

364 calories; 14 grams fat; 35% calories from fat; 939 mg. sodium

Bang Bang Chicken

Food vendors in China call attention to this dish by banging two sticks together.

1-2 **tablespoons peanut oil**
1 **whole, boneless, skinless chicken breast, cut into strips**
1 **clove garlic, minced**
2 **teaspoons grated ginger root**
1 **green onion, chopped into 1-inch pieces**
¼ **cup water**
2 **tablespoons soy sauce**
2 **tablespoons peanut butter**
1 **tablespoon red wine vinegar**
1 **cup broccoli florets**
1 **cucumber, sliced**
1 **cup grated carrots**
¼ **cup finely chopped peanuts**
  white rice, cooked

- Heat oil in wok or sauté pan. Stir-fry chicken, garlic, ginger and green onion until chicken is cooked through.

- Add water, soy sauce, peanut butter and vinegar. Simmer 5 minutes.

- Add broccoli and cucumber and simmer until vegetables are crisp tender, about 6 minutes.

- Add grated carrots and cook 1 minute.

- Serve over hot, prepared rice. Garnish with finely chopped peanuts.

Yields 4 servings.

Chinese Chicken with Long Rice

3 pounds boneless, skinless chicken breasts

6 tablespoons soy sauce, divided

1 tablespoon sesame oil

2 tablespoons minced fresh ginger

3 cloves garlic, minced

1½ teaspoons sugar

⅛ teaspoon pepper

20 dried shiitake mushrooms

6-8 green onions

10 ounces long rice (rice sticks)

2 tablespoons vegetable oil

½ cup chicken broth

cilantro sprigs for garnish

- Cut chicken into strips ½-inch thick and 3 inches long.

- Combine 2 tablespoons soy sauce, sesame oil, ginger, garlic, sugar and pepper. Add chicken and mix well. Cover. Refrigerate 15-60 minutes.

- Cover dried mushrooms with hot water. Let stand until soft, about 20 minutes. Drain. Cut off and discard stems. Reserve 3 or 4 mushrooms for garnish. Cut remaining ones into thin slivers. Set aside.

- Cut green onions into 2-inch lengths. Set aside.

- Bring 3-4 quarts of water to a boil in a large pot. Remove from heat. Add long rice and let stand until soft, about 3 minutes. Drain.

- Place large skillet over high heat. When hot, add vegetable oil and marinated chicken. Cook, stirring, until meat turns white on surface, about 2 minutes. Reduce heat to low and add mushrooms, green onions, long rice, chicken broth and 4 tablespoons soy sauce. Cover and simmer, stirring occasionally, until hot, about 3 minutes.

- Garnish with reserved mushrooms and cilantro.

Yields 12 servings.

Chicken Asparagus Stir-Fry

1 whole boneless, skinless chicken breast

1 pound asparagus

2 tablespoons peanut oil, divided

2 cloves garlic, minced

½ cup chicken broth

1 teaspoon sherry

2 teaspoons soy sauce

2 teaspoons cornstarch

2 teaspoons cold water

¼ teaspoon sugar

2 tablespoons toasted sesame seeds

- Cut chicken breast into thin strips.

- Snap bottoms of asparagus. Wash thoroughly. Slice diagonally, leaving tips whole.

- Heat wok. Add 1 tablespoon oil and garlic. Add asparagus and stir-fry 30 seconds. Remove asparagus and garlic from pan and set aside.

- Reheat pan and add remaining oil. Add chicken and stir-fry 1 minute. Add chicken broth, sherry and soy sauce. Cook 2-3 minutes until chicken is done. Add asparagus and stir-fry with chicken 1 minute.

- Blend cornstarch and water. Add to chicken-asparagus mixture and stir until thickened.

- Sprinkle with sugar and sesame seeds before serving.

Yields 2-3 servings.

379 calories; 21 grams fat; 49% calories from fat; 648 mg. sodium

Grilled Breast of Chicken with Pasta and Champagne Cream Sauce

6 boneless, skinless chicken breast halves

2 1-pound boxes linguine (cook as instructed on box)

- Marinate chicken in marinade for 1 hour. Broil or grill chicken breasts.

Marinade

¼ cup soy sauce

3 cloves garlic, crushed

1 teaspoon thyme

1 teaspoon basil

½ cup champagne

3 tablespoons olive oil

¼ teaspoon black pepper

Champagne Cream Sauce

1 tablespoon olive oil

1 tablespoon chopped shallot

¼ cup diced onion

¼ cup champagne

1 tablespoon butter

⅛ cup flour

2 cups chicken stock

2 cups heavy cream

salt and pepper, to taste

1 teaspoon chicken base or bouillon

- Heat oil and sauté shallot and onion. Add champagne and cook until mixture is reduced by half. Add butter and flour and cook for 3 minutes. Add chicken stock and heavy cream. Reduce heat to low-medium and cook for 10 minutes. Add salt, pepper and chicken bouillon for flavor.

- Slice chicken. Place pasta on platter, add cream sauce and chicken.

Yield 6 servings.

Parmesan-Encrusted Opakapaka

½ cup grated Parmesan cheese
½ cup panko flakes or bread crumbs
 salt and pepper, to taste
2 tablespoons melted butter
2 tablespoons olive oil
4 opakapaka fillets (any mild, medium-firm fish such as halibut)

- Combine cheese, panko, salt and pepper. Add melted butter and mix well.

- Place mixture on each fish fillet and press out evenly on both sides.

- Chill in refrigerator 1-2 hours so crust will harden.

- Preheat oven to 350°.

- Heat sauté pan until very hot. Add olive oil. Sauté fillets until golden brown.

- Finish cooking in oven 8-15 minutes, depending on thickness of fillets, until fish flakes easily.

Yields 4 servings.

Grilled Salmon with Maui Onion Relish

2 large Maui onions
¼ cup olive oil
1½ tablespoons sugar
1 bay leaf
1 teaspoon chopped fresh thyme
1½ tablespoons balsamic vinegar
4 salmon steaks
 mayonnaise

- Preheat grill.

- Prepare relish. Sauté onions in oil until soft. Add sugar and herbs. Cook until onions are caramelized. Add vinegar.

- Lightly brush mayonnaise on both sides of salmon. Grill steaks. Serve with relish.

Yields 4 servings.

Salmon (New Brunswick Salmon) Quiche

Crust

- 1 cup flour
- 1 teaspoon sugar
- ½ teaspoon salt
- ½ cup grated cheddar cheese
- ⅓ cup vegetable oil
- 2 tablespoons milk

- Mix crust ingredients together. Take out ¼ cup and set aside. Line bottom and sides of pie plate with remaining crust mixture.

Filling

- 8 ounces smoked salmon, sliced into pieces
- 2 eggs, beaten
- ¾ cup milk
- ¼ teaspoon salt
- ⅛ teaspoon black pepper
- 1 tablespoon white vinegar paprika, to garnish

- Preheat oven to 400°.
- Combine filling ingredients. Pour into shell. Top with reserved crust mixture. Sprinkle with paprika.
- Bake at 400° 15 minutes. Immediately reduce heat to 350° and bake ½ hour. Allow to set 20 minutes before cutting.

Yields 6 servings.

Note: Recipe is easily doubled.

Variation: Add some, or all, of the following ingredients:

- ½ cup sautéed mushrooms
- ¼ cup chopped onion
- 3 tablespoons capers
- 2 tablespoons chopped fresh cilantro

Salmon Encroûte

1 17¼-ounce package frozen
   puff pastry, thawed
   flour
1 pound salmon fillet,
   skinned and deboned
1 tablespoon mayonnaise
1 teaspoon Dijon mustard
1 tablespoon capers
3 green onions, chopped
1 teaspoon chopped fresh
   dill (optional)
1 egg white

- Preheat oven to 375°.

- Sprinkle flour on cutting board. Roll out pastry with rolling pin to fit salmon. Cut salmon to smaller pieces if necessary. Place salmon on pastry.

- Spread mayonnaise and Dijon mustard on salmon, topping with capers and green onion. Fold pastry dough to cover salmon and seal with egg white.

- Keep in refrigerator until ready to bake. Mix a little water with egg white and brush on pastry before baking.

- Bake 15 minutes.

Yields 4 servings.

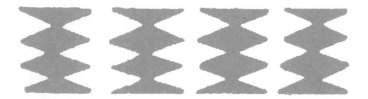

Filet of Fish with Macadamia Nuts

2 swordfish filets
salt and white pepper
1 egg yolk
4 tablespoons coarsely
ground macadamia nuts
1 tablespoon chopped
parsley
butter or olive oil for
sautéing
2 tablespoons clarified
butter
⅛ cup dry sherry
juice of ¼ lemon

- Season fish filets with salt and pepper. Brush filets with egg yolk and press nuts into both sides of fish. Sprinkle with parsley.
- Sauté fish in butter or oil 3 minutes on each side. Remove from pan and keep warm.
- Add clarified butter, sherry and lemon juice to pan drippings. Heat and pour over fish. Serve at once.

Yields 2 servings.

Grilled Salmon with Arugula

1 4-pound slab Atlantic
salmon
olive oil
Hawaiian salt or coarse
salt
pepper
fresh oregano, to taste
fresh basil, to taste
2 limes, divided
¼ pound arugula

- Preheat grill or broiler.
- Rub salmon with oil. Sprinkle with salt, pepper and herbs. Squeeze juice of 1 lime over top.
- Broil or grill one side only, about 10 minutes per inch of thickness of salmon. Do not overcook.
- Remove to serving platter.
- Drizzle arugula with olive oil and juice of second lime. Cover salmon with arugula. Serve.

Yields 8-12 servings.

Variation: Watercress may be substituted for arugula.

Chinese Steamed Salmon

1 whole (5-pound) salmon
1 cup chopped chung choi
   (salted turnip)
1½ cups cilantro leaves, torn
   into pieces
½ cup chopped fresh ginger
   root
¾ cup chopped green onion
¾ cup soy sauce
½ cup peanut oil, heated
   white rice

- Steam or poach salmon 25-30 minutes. Remove to heated platter.
- Sprinkle chung choi, cilantro, ginger and onion over fish. Pour soy sauce over fish followed by heated oil.
- Serve with white rice.

Yields 10-12 servings.

Variation: Substitute onaga, kumu or mullet for salmon.

Easy Baked Salmon Steaks

4 salmon steaks
   salt and pepper, to taste
¼ cup melted butter
2 tablespoons lemon juice
3 teaspoons minced onion
   paprika for garnish

- Preheat oven to 350°.
- Sprinkle both sides of salmon with salt and pepper.
- Mix together melted butter, lemon juice and onion. Dip salmon into mixture.
- Arrange on baking dish and pour remaining butter sauce over steaks.
- Bake 25-30 minutes or until easily flaked with fork but still moist.
- Sprinkle with paprika and serve.

Yields 4 servings.

Zesty Shrimp with Vegetables

¼ teaspoon crushed red pepper

¼ teaspoon dried basil

¼ teaspoon dried thyme

¼ teaspoon dried oregano

¼ teaspoon salt

¼ teaspoon pepper

8 tablespoons olive oil, divided

¼ cup finely chopped green onion

1 clove garlic, minced

¾ pound mushrooms, thinly sliced

2 small zucchini, cut into quarter-inch rounds and then halved

1 pound shrimp, peeled and deveined

½ cup chardonnay
steamed rice

- Combine red pepper, basil, thyme, oregano, salt and pepper. Set aside.

- Pour 4 tablespoons oil in sauté pan. Add onion and garlic and sauté briefly. Stir in mushrooms and zucchini and cook 3-4 minutes. Add shrimp and seasoning mix.

- Cook, shaking and tossing ingredients, 3-4 minutes or until shrimp are barely pink.

- Pour in chardonnay and cook over medium high heat until liquid is reduced to ¼ cup. Add remaining 4 tablespoons oil, 1 tablespoon at a time, stirring constantly. Sauce will thicken slightly.

- Serve over steamed rice.

Yields 2 servings.

Rosemary Scallops

4 12-inch-long rosemary branches or 10-inch bamboo skewers
1 teaspoon chopped fresh rosemary leaves
½ teaspoon Hawaiian salt
¼ teaspoon paprika
⅛ teaspoon cayenne
16 medium sea scallops (about ¾ pound)
2 tablespoons olive oil

- Preheat grill.
- Remove leaves from all but top 3 inches of each rosemary branch. Soak branches or skewers in water for 30 minutes.
- Stir together chopped rosemary, salt, paprika and cayenne in small bowl.
- Using knife or spoon, remove tough muscle from side of each scallop if necessary.
- Pat scallops dry with paper towel. Sprinkle scallops with rosemary mixture. Thread 4 scallops onto each rosemary branch or bamboo skewer.
- Brush scallops with oil.
- Grill over moderately high heat 1-2 minutes on each side or until golden and just cooked through.

Yields 4 servings.

114 calories; 7 grams fat; 58% calories from fat; 387 mg. sodium

Grilling is a high heat method where tender foods are cooked quickly over the flame of a very hot fire and benefit from the smoke of the coals.

Barbecuing is cooking tough cuts of meat over the smoke and indirect heat of a very low fire for a long time.

Seared Scallops

1 pound large sea scallops, patted dry
1 tablespoon olive oil
Sauce

- Pour oil in non-stick skillet large enough to hold scallops in one layer. Heat oil over high heat until hot but not smoking. Sear scallops for 1-2 minutes on each side or until just cooked through and golden brown. Using a slotted spoon, transfer scallops to plate and cover loosely to keep warm.

Sauce

1½ tablespoons olive oil
2 cloves garlic, thinly sliced
1 tomato, diced
⅛ teaspoon dried thyme, crumbled
¼ teaspoon Hawaiian salt
¼ teaspoon dried red pepper flakes
1 tablespoon butter
¼ cup shredded fresh basil leaves

- Heat oil in skillet, add garlic and cook, stirring, until it changes color.
- Add tomato and thyme and cook mixture for 1 minute.
- Season with salt and pepper flakes. Add butter and simmer 2 minutes.
- Spoon mixture over and around scallops and sprinkle with basil.

Yields 2-4 servings.

Variation: Substitute cleaned, deveined shrimp for scallops. Sauce is also good on fish.

Broiled Sea Scallops

½ cup dry vermouth
1 tablespoon vegetable oil
½ teaspoon salt
1 clove garlic, crushed
2 tablespoons chopped
  parsley
1½ pounds sea scallops cut
  into bite-size pieces
1 tablespoon butter
½ cup bread crumbs
  paprika

- Preheat broiler.
- Mix vermouth, oil, salt, garlic and parsley to create a marinade. Marinate scallops for 1 hour in refrigerator.
- Melt butter and toss with bread crumbs.
- Place scallops and marinade in individual, ovenproof shallow baking dishes. Place 4 inches from broiler heat and broil 2 minutes. Turn scallops. Sprinkle with buttered bread crumbs and paprika. Broil 2 more minutes and serve.

Yields 4 servings.

Baked Salmon with Fresh Vegetables

1 3-pound salmon,
  butterflied, or 6 salmon
  steaks
¾ cup mayonnaise
1 large Maui onion, diced
2 large tomatoes, diced
½ pound fresh mushrooms,
  diced
¼ cup smoked bacon, diced,
  cooked
2 tablespoons capers
  juice from ½ lemon
  salt and pepper

- Preheat oven to 425°. Lightly coat baking dish with nonstick cooking spray.
- Rinse salmon and pat dry. Place salmon skin side down in baking dish. Spread mayonnaise evenly over entire fish.
- Sprinkle diced onion, tomatoes, mushrooms, bacon and capers on salmon. Squeeze lemon juice over fish. Salt and pepper to taste. Cover salmon tightly with foil.
- Bake 35-45 minutes, or until vegetables are slightly cooked and fish is tender.

Yields 6 servings.

Tequila Swordfish

Garlic-Rosemary Butter

2 whole heads garlic
¼ cup water
   branch fresh rosemary,
   about 1 tablespoon
½ cup unsalted butter,
   softened

- Preheat oven to 350°.
- Place garlic, water and rosemary in small roasting pan. Cover with foil.
- Bake 45 minutes. Remove foil and bake 5 more minutes to toast rosemary.
- Finely chop rosemary leaves. Separate garlic cloves and squeeze out pulp. Mix rosemary and garlic with butter. Butter can be made ahead.

Swordfish

4-5 6-ounce swordfish steaks
   salt
   cornmeal with black
   pepper, to taste
¼ cup olive oil
6 tomatillos, husked and
   thinly sliced into wedges
½ cup tequila
½ cup chicken stock
6 teaspoons lime juice
1 lime cut into wedges for
   garnish
   cilantro sprigs for garnish

- Season swordfish with salt and dredge in cornmeal.
- Heat olive oil in large sauté pan. Add fish. Cook about 4 minutes, until nicely browned. Turn, and cook until done. Place on warm platter.
- Pour off excess oil from pan. Add sliced tomatillos and brown slightly, about 2 minutes. Deglaze pan with tequila. Add chicken stock and lime juice. Stir in ¼ cup of Garlic-Rosemary Butter. Adjust seasoning.
- Spoon sauce over fish and garnish with cilantro sprigs and lime wedges.

Yields 4 servings.

Note: Leftover Garlic-Rosemary Butter can be used to roast potatoes or top baked potatoes.

Steamed Clams

2-3 **pounds clams**
  ¼ **cup white wine**
  ½ **cup water**
  ¼ **cup butter**
   juice of 1 lemon or 1 lime
  1 **clove garlic**
   melted butter
   French bread

- Thoroughly wash clams by covering them with water and letting them stand 15 minutes. Rinse with running cold water for 1-2 minutes.

- Place wine, water, butter, lemon juice and garlic in large pot and bring to boil.

- Add clams, cover tightly, and steam just until shells open, about 5-8 minutes. Discard unopened clams.

- Serve clams with melted butter.

- The remaining wine-butter broth may be poured into individual cups and served with warm French bread.

Yields 2-4 servings.

798 calories; 31 grams fat; 35% calories from fat; 668 mg. sodium

Seared Ahi with Honey Mustard Sauce

Ahi

**8 ahi steaks, ¾- to 1-inch
    thick
mayonnaise
blackened spices
Honey Mustard Sauce**

- Preheat grill or broiler to 400°.

- Spread thin layer of mayonnaise on each side of steak. Sprinkle both sides with blackened spices.

- Grill steaks 2 minutes on one side, turn and cook 1 minute more. (Do not overcook. Center should be red or rare like sashimi; if not, shorten cooking time.)

- Slice steaks, across the grain. Drizzle with Honey Mustard Sauce.

Honey Mustard Sauce

**1 cup Dijon mustard
½ cup mayonnaise
1 teaspoon horseradish
1 tablespoon soy sauce
3 tablespoons honey
1 teaspoon sesame oil**

- Combine all ingredients and mix well. Set aside.

Yields 1¾ cups sauce.

Lomi Salmon

½ pound salted salmon
1 large white onion or 6
   green onions, thinly
   sliced
6 large tomatoes, diced
8 ice cubes
   lemon slices

- Remove bone and skin from salmon, soak in cold water 3-4 hours. Change water every hour. Drain water.

- Shred salmon into small pieces with fingers or spoon. Add onion and tomatoes. Massage this mixture with hands until everything is broken up. Add ice cubes and chill.

- Garnish with lemon slices.

Yields 4-5 servings.

Variation: If unsalted salmon is used, rub salmon with rock salt and let stand overnight. Rinse completely and soak in water 1 hour or more, changing water 2-3 times.

Note: Lomi means massage in Hawaiian.

Red Snapper with Vermouth Cream Sauce

1 cup dry vermouth
1 medium onion, chopped
¾ cup whipping cream
2 quarter-size pieces ginger, chopped
1 clove garlic, chopped
1 teaspoon soy sauce
   salt and pepper, to taste
½ cup butter, cut into pieces; 1 tablespoon butter
1 teaspoon cornstarch
2 pounds red snapper
1 bunch watercress, chopped

- Combine vermouth and onion in saucepan. Bring to boil and cook until reduced by half.

- Add cream and heat slowly. Strain and return liquid to pan. Add ginger, garlic, soy sauce, salt and pepper. Add butter pieces, stirring after each addition.

- Dissolve cornstarch in small amount of cold water and add to sauce. Mix well.

- Sauté snapper in 1 tablespoon butter until done (3 minutes on each side).

- Place snapper on chopped watercress. Top with sauce and serve.

Yields 6 servings.

Grilled Seafood Brochettes

Brochettes

8 large shrimp, peeled and deveined

8 sea scallops

½ pound fresh tuna, cut into 8 pieces

Marinade

½ large green bell pepper, cut into ½-inch piece

2 small onions, cut in ½-inch thick wedges

8 cherry tomatoes

lemon wedges

Marinade

½ cup olive oil

2 tablespoons fresh lemon juice

1 clove garlic, minced

1 teaspoon ground ginger

¼ teaspoon salt

¼ teaspoon black pepper

- Rinse shrimp, scallops and tuna and pat dry. Add to marinade and toss until all seafood is coated

- Chill 1-2 hours.

- Preheat grill or broiler.

- Thread seafood, bell peppers, onions and tomatoes onto skewers.

- Grill or broil brochettes about 3 minutes on each side. Garnish with lemon wedges.

- Whisk together all marinade ingredients.

Yields 4 servings.

202 calories; 5 grams fat; 24% calories from fat; 194 mg. sodium

Accompaniments

Pineapple Iced Tea

6 tea bags
¼ cup sugar
4 cups boiling water
bunch fresh mint
juice of 3 lemons
5 tablespoons pineapple
juice
fresh pineapple spears to
garnish
fresh mint leaves to
garnish

- Place tea bags and sugar in 2-quart pitcher. Add 4 cups boiling water. Steep 15 minutes. Remove tea bags.

- Steep fresh mint leaves in tea at least 3 minutes and remove. Add lemon and pineapple juices. Fill pitcher with cold water.

- Serve over ice. Garnish with pineapple and mint.

Yields 2 quarts.

'Old Plantation' Iced Tea

7 tea bags or ½ cup loose
tea
12½ cups water, divided
2 bunches mint
2 cups sugar
juice of 5-6 lemons

- Bring 12 cups water to boil; add tea. Let steep a few minutes before removing tea.

- Toss in handful of mint.

- Bring ½ cup water and sugar to boil and add to hot tea. Let stand several hours. Remove mint. Add lemon juice. Chill and serve over ice cubes.

Yields 14 servings.

Ginger-Grapefruit Punch (Non-Alcoholic)

2 quarts grapefruit soda
(or 2 cups sweetened
grapefruit juice mixed
with 6 cups soda water),
divided
2 quarts chilled tea
5 ounces orange juice
concentrate, defrosted
2 inches fresh ginger root,
peeled and pressed to
yield 1 teaspoon ginger
juice
garnish with mint, orange
slices and/or fresh or
reconstituted cranberries

Tea

1 tablespoon green tea
leaves or any other tea
leaves
2 quarts boiling water
poured over tea leaves or
2 quarts any instant tea,
chilled thoroughly
2 tablespoons sugar

Night Before - Prepare Ice Block

- Freeze 1 quart grapefruit soda
in round mixing bowl (diameter
smaller than punchbowl).

Next Day

- Pour 1 quart chilled grapefruit
soda into 5- to 6-quart punchbowl.

- Stir in chilled tea, orange juice
concentrate and ginger juice.

- Add grapefruit-soda-flavored
ice block.

- Garnish with mint, orange
slices and/or fresh or reconstituted dried cranberries.

- Steep 5 minutes and strain.
Stir in sugar. Chill thoroughly.

Yields 4 quarts.

Banana-Mango Smoothie

4-6 ripe bananas
  2 ripe mangoes
  1 tablespoon honey
  3 ice cubes
  ¼ cup apple juice or coconut
    milk

- Blend ingredients together until smooth.

Yields 2-3 glasses.

Rum Punch

1 48-ounce can pineapple
   juice
2 6-ounce cans frozen
   lemonade
1 48-ounce can orange juice
1 10-ounce jar maraschino
   cherries, drained and
   halved
1 6-ounce can mandarin
   oranges, drained
3 1-liter bottles ginger ale
5 cups rum

- Combine all ingredients. Mix well.

Yields 25 servings.

Variation: Omit rum. Freeze fruit juice and ginger ale combination for delicious frozen pops.

Chichi

¾ ounce coconut syrup
¾ ounce pineapple juice
¾ ounce sweet-and-sour
   lemon juice
¾ ounce half and half
2 ounces vodka
¼ lime, squeezed
  ice

- Mix all ingredients together with handful of ice in blender.
- Fill 14-ounce glass. Add ice to keep cold.

Yields 1 serving.

Variation: Omit vodka to make a nice coconut milkshake.

Mai Tai

Hawaii's favorite cocktail.

1 46-ounce can
  unsweetened pineapple
  juice
4 ounces fresh lemon juice
1½ tablespoons frozen guava
  juice
1 cup dark rum
½ cup Lemon Hart Rum
½ cup West Indies Rum
1 cup orange Curaçao

- Combine pineapple, lemon and guava juices.
- Add rums and Curaçao. Serve in cocktail glasses over ice.

Yields 15-20 servings.

George Bunton's Hawaiian Mai Tai

1 ounce light rum
1 ounce dark rum
½ ounce orange Curaçao
½ ounce Orgeat syrup
½-1 ounce simple syrup
  juice of ½ lemon
  juice of ½ lime
1 teaspoon frozen guava
  nectar concentrate
  pineapple spear
  maraschino cherry
  orange wedge
½ ounce Jamaican rum
1 ounce pineapple juice,
  optional

- Mix all ingredients in large "Mai Tai" glass over coarsely crushed ice. More lime juice may be used with proportional increase in simple syrup.
- Garnish with pineapple spear, cherry and orange wedge. Float Jamaican rum on top of drink. Do not stir. Sip from bottom with straw.

Yields 1 serving.

Prune Crackseed

This is an island favorite.

6 12-ounce packages
   seedless prunes
10 whole cloves
1 tablespoon Chinese 5
   spice
1 16-ounce box dark brown
   sugar
3 tablespoons Hawaiian salt
   (rock salt)
3 tablespoons whiskey
1½ cups lemon juice
1 8-ounce package seedless
   li hing mui (Chinese
   seasoning)
1 3-ounce package lemon
   peel (optional)
1 6-ounce package dried
   apricots (optional)

- Mix all ingredients together in large gallon jug. Cover.
- Let flavors permeate about 4 days.
- Occasionally roll jug back and forth to redistribute ingredients.
- Enjoy as snack.

Yields 1 gallon.

Corn Relish

2 cups fresh or frozen whole
   kernel corn
½ cup finely diced red onion
2 plum tomatoes, diced
1 fresh jalapeño pepper,
   seeded and chopped
¼ cup lime juice
1 cup diced jicama
2 avocados, diced
1 cup canned black beans
⅓ cup chopped cilantro

- Thaw corn and dry.
- In large bowl, mix corn, onion, tomatoes, pepper, lime juice, jicama, avocados and beans.
- Refrigerate up to 4 hours. Toss in cilantro just before serving.

Yields 4-8 servings.

Mango Papaya Salsa

This salsa is great for broiled fish or chicken.

1 fresh or frozen mango,
   diced
1 cup diced fresh papaya
½ cup diced red bell pepper
½ cup diced yellow pepper
1 tablespoon finely chopped
   fresh jalapeño pepper
2 tablespoons minced fresh
   cilantro
2½ tablespoons fresh lime
   juice
   salt, to taste

- Mix all ingredients together.

Yields 3 cups.

Mango Chutney

1 quart vinegar
7 cups sugar
1 cup raisins
1 cup ginger, chopped
2 Hawaiian chili peppers,
   chopped and seeded
5 cloves garlic
3 tablespoons salt
4 cloves
½ teaspoon allspice
   juice of 1 lemon
10 cups half ripe mangoes,
   sliced

- Combine all ingredients, except mangoes, in large pan. Mix well. Bring to boil. Continue to boil gently for 45 minutes, stirring frequently.

- Add mangoes and simmer 10 minutes until glazed. Process in jars or refrigerate.

Yields 4 quarts.

Mangonaise

Great sauce for grilled meats and vegetables or use as a sandwich spread.

1 ripe mango
1 clove garlic
½ cup macadamia nut oil
2 teaspoons lemon juice
salt and pepper, to taste

- Blend mango and garlic in food processor. Add oil slowly. Add lemon juice.

Yields 1 cup.

Variation: Use any light-flavored oil.

Fresh Fruit Salsa

Serve this salsa over grilled fish, spooned over cream cheese or with a basket of cinnamon-flavored crisps, crackers or tortillas.

1 medium orange, peeled, membranes removed and finely chopped
2 large kiwis, peeled and finely chopped
½ cup finely chopped fresh pineapple
1 ripe peach or nectarine, peeled and finely chopped
¼ cup thinly sliced green onion
¼ cup finely chopped yellow or green bell pepper
1 tablespoon fresh lemon or lime juice
1 fresh jalapeño pepper, seeded and chopped
1 cup finely chopped strawberries

- Combine orange, kiwis, pineapple, peach, onion, pepper, juice and jalapeño pepper. Cover. Chill 6-24 hours.
- Stir in strawberries just before serving.

Yields 3 cups.

Note: Chop ingredients by hand for best texture and prettiest appearance.

Peanut Satay Sauce

⅓ cup unsalted dry roasted
    peanuts
    salt, to taste
1 small shallot
1 clove garlic
¼ cup top quality peanut
    butter
6 tablespoons coconut milk
2 tablespoons peanut oil
1 teaspoon sugar
½ teaspoon Chinese chili oil
¼ teaspoon ground cumin
¼ teaspoon ground
    coriander

- Place peanuts in food processor. Process until peanuts are minced. Remove 2 tablespoons and set aside. Continue processing peanuts until mixture becomes peanut butter. Add salt to taste. Quickly blend. Remove from processor and set aside.

- In food processor, finely chop shallot and garlic.

- Add peanut butter, coconut milk, oil, sugar, chili oil, cumin and coriander. Process until very smooth, about 20 seconds. Sauce should be consistency of very rich cream.

- Before serving, sprinkle reserved nuts over sauce. Serve with grilled or broiled, skewered chicken, beef or shrimp.

Yields 1¼ cups.

Note: Sauce may be refrigerated up to 3 days. Bring to room temperature and stir vigorously before serving. Add a little peanut oil or water to thin sauce, if needed.

Pam's Salsa

2 Anaheim peppers, seeded, deveined and finely chopped

2 jalapeño peppers, seeded, deveined and finely chopped

2 tomatoes, peeled and finely chopped

1 bunch green onions (tops also), finely chopped

½ bunch cilantro leaves, chopped

2 tablespoons vinegar

1 tablespoon olive oil

salt and pepper to taste

- Wash and chop all vegetables. Place in bowl and chill.
- Just before serving, add vinegar, olive oil, salt and pepper.
- Serve as a condiment.

Mango Cucumber Salsa

Try this tasty contrast of mango and cucumber flavors.

1 firm ripe small mango

⅓ Japanese cucumber

2 tablespoons finely chopped scallion

1 teaspoon fresh lime juice

½ teaspoon extra-virgin olive oil

½ seeded jalapeño pepper, finely chopped

- Peel mango and cut flesh from pit. Dice mango into ¼-inch pieces and transfer to small bowl. Halve and seed cucumber. Dice cucumber into ¼-inch pieces and add to mango. Stir in chopped scallion, lime juice and olive oil until well combined. Season with salt and pepper. Serve with fish or chicken.

Yields 2 servings.

Kit's Chicken Barbecue Sauce

¼ cup white vinegar
½ cup water
2 tablespoons sugar
1 tablespoon Dijon mustard
   thick slice lemon (rind
   and all)
1 onion, sliced
¼ cup butter
   salt and pepper, to taste
½ cup ketchup
2 tablespoons
   Worcestershire sauce

- Mix vinegar, water, sugar, mustard, lemon, onion, butter, salt and pepper. Simmer 20 minutes uncovered. Add extra water as needed while cooking the onions.

- Add ketchup and Worcestershire. Bring to boil. Baste grilled chicken with sauce before serving.

Yields 1 cup.

Beer-Be-Que Sauce

1 cup beer
½ teaspoon salt
1 cup ketchup
⅓ cup vinegar
⅓ cup brown sugar
3 tablespoons
   Worcestershire sauce
1 teaspoon dry mustard
1 teaspoon paprika
½ teaspoon chili powder
1 medium onion, thinly
   sliced
½ lemon, thinly sliced

- Combine beer, salt, ketchup, vinegar, sugar, Worcestershire, mustard, paprika and chili powder in saucepan. Bring to boil. Cook and stir 5 minutes. Add onion and lemon.

- Spoon or brush over ribs, burgers, chicken, etc.

Yields 2½ cups sauce.

Variation: Use extra sauce for making sloppy joes (mix sauce with browned ground beef, serve on buns).

DESSERTS

Desserts

Kimi's Famous Fresh Strawberry Cake

This cake is not only delicious but beautiful as well.

1 18.5-ounce package white cake mix
¼ cup flour
1 cup vegetable oil
½ cup water or milk
4 eggs
1 3-ounce package strawberry gelatin
1 cup chopped fresh strawberries, drained

- Preheat oven to 350°. Oil and flour tube or bundt pan.

- Combine cake mix, flour, oil, water (or milk), eggs and strawberry gelatin in large mixing bowl. Beat at medium speed 3-4 minutes. Fold in strawberries. Pour into prepared pan.

- Bake 55-60 minutes.

Strawberry Frosting

½ cup butter, softened
¾-1 pound powdered sugar
¾ cup chopped fresh strawberries, drained
5-7 whole strawberries for garnishing

- Cream butter and sugar until light and fluffy. Slowly add strawberries. Beat at high speed until smooth.

- Use immediately. Garnish cake with whole or halved strawberries.

Yields 15-20 servings.

Mango Cake

1½ cups sugar
1½ cups vegetable oil
 4 eggs
 2 cups flour
 1 teaspoon baking powder
 1 teaspoon cinnamon
 ¼ teaspoon salt
 2 cups shredded or chopped
   half-ripe mango (about 3
   mangoes)
½ cup chopped, roasted
   macadamia nuts
   powdered sugar

- Preheat oven to 350°. Grease and flour 13x9-inch baking pan.

- Combine sugar and oil. Add eggs, one at a time.

- Combine flour, baking powder, cinnamon and salt. Add to egg mixture. Add mango and nuts. Pour into prepared pan.

- Bake 55 minutes. Let cool in pan.

- Sprinkle with sifted powdered sugar before serving.

Yields 20 servings.

To peel a mango, stand it on end and, using a sharp knife, cut along central pit and remove flesh from one side. Repeat for all four sides. Score each mango quarter lengthwise into thin slices and remove from the peel.

Pumpkin Cake

3 cups flour
2 teaspoons baking powder
2 teaspoons baking soda
1 teaspoon salt
2 teaspoons cinnamon
1 teaspoon nutmeg
1 teaspoon ginger
4 eggs
2 cups sugar
2 cups cooked, puréed
   pumpkin
1¼ cups vegetable oil
½ cup nuts, chopped,
   optional
   powdered sugar

- Preheat oven to 350°. Grease and flour large tube pan or 2 loaf pans.
- In medium mixing bowl, sift together flour, baking powder, baking soda, salt, cinnamon, nutmeg and ginger.
- In large mixing bowl, beat eggs. Add sugar and beat well. Blend in pumpkin and oil.
- Add in flour mixture, beating well until batter is smooth. Add nuts.
- Bake in tube pan 1 hour, or 2 loaf pans 50 minutes.
- Dust with powdered sugar before serving.

Yields 15-20 servings.

Pineapple Carrot Cake

The pineapple puts this cake over the top.

2 cups sifted flour
2 teaspoons baking soda
1 teaspoon salt
2 teaspoons cinnamon
2 cups sugar
4 eggs
1 cup vegetable oil
2 cups grated carrots
1 8-ounce can crushed pineapple
¾ cup chopped nuts
Frosting

- Preheat oven to 350°.
- Sift together flour, baking soda, salt and cinnamon.
- Combine sugar, eggs and oil, mixing well. Stir in dry ingredients. Add carrots, pineapple and nuts. Pour into ungreased 9x13-inch pan.
- Bake 35-40 minutes.
- When cool, spread with cream cheese frosting.

Frosting

1 8-ounce package cream cheese
½ cup butter
1 teaspoon vanilla
8 ounces powdered sugar, sifted

- Beat cream cheese until fluffy. Cream butter into cream cheese and add vanilla. Stir in powdered sugar and beat well until frosting becomes smooth and easy to spread on cooled cake.

Yields 20 servings.

Cherry Brandy Cake

2 7.5-ounce containers
  glazed cherries
6 cups sifted flour, divided
2 cups butter
2⅔ cups sugar
8 extra large eggs
1 teaspoon baking powder
¼ teaspoon salt
2 tablespoons brandy

- Preheat oven to 300°. Line 4 8x4-inch pans with waxed paper or parchment paper. Do not grease.

- Cut each cherry into 6-8 pieces. Stir cherries with 2 cups flour. Set aside.

- Cream butter. Add sugar gradually, mixing well. Add eggs, one at a time. Beat well after each addition.

- Sift together 4 cups flour, baking powder and salt. Fold half into creamed mixture. Add brandy. Fold in other half of flour mixture and then cherries with flour.

- Spoon batter into pans.

- Bake 1 hour.

Yields 12-16 servings.

Chocolate Rum Cake

1 cup chopped pecans or
  walnuts
1 18.5 ounce package
  chocolate cake mix
1 3.9-ounce package instant
  chocolate pudding mix
2 heaping tablespoons
  unsweetened cocoa
  powder
4 eggs
½ cup milk
½ cup vegetable oil
½ cup dark rum
½ cup chocolate chips,
  optional
  Glaze

Glaze

½ cup butter
½ cup brown sugar
½ cup dark rum

- Preheat oven to 350°. Grease and flour bundt pan.
- Sprinkle nuts over bottom of pan.
- Combine cake mix, pudding mix, cocoa powder, eggs, milk, oil and rum. Beat with electric mixer at medium speed 3 minutes. Add chocolate chips, if you wish. Pour batter over nuts.
- Bake 50-60 minutes.
- While cake is still warm, prick top and slowly drizzle glaze evenly over surface. Allow cake to absorb glaze.

- Melt butter in saucepan. Add sugar. Bring to boil. Boil 2 minutes, stirring constantly. Remove from heat. Stir in rum.

Yields 15-20 servings.

Note: Delicious when served warm (brings out rum flavor) with vanilla ice cream.

Double-Rich Chocolate Cake

1 18.5-ounce package
   chocolate cake mix
1 3.9-ounce package
   chocolate instant
   pudding mix
4 eggs
¾ cup water
½ cup sour cream
¼ cup oil
1 cup semisweet chocolate
   chips
   powdered sugar for
   garnish

- Preheat oven to 350°. Grease and flour 10-inch tube pan.

- Combine cake mix, pudding mix, eggs, water, sour cream and oil in large mixing bowl. Beat 4 minutes on medium speed with electric mixer. Stir in chocolate chips. Pour into prepared pan.

- Bake 55-60 minutes or until cake springs back when lightly pressed. (Caution: Do not underbake.) Cool in pan 15 minutes. Remove and finish cooling on rack.

- Sprinkle with powdered sugar.

Yields 15-20 servings.

Variation: Bake in 13x9-inch pan 45-50 minutes until done.

Orange Date Cake

2   cups sifted cake flour
1¼ cups sugar, divided
1   teaspoon baking soda
1   teaspoon baking powder
1   cup chopped dates
½   cup chopped nuts
1   cup butter, melted and
     cooled
2   eggs, well-beaten
⅔   cup buttermilk
3   medium oranges

- Preheat oven to 350°. Grease and flour 8x8-inch cake pan.

- Combine flour, 1 cup sugar, baking soda, baking powder, dates and nuts. Add melted butter, eggs and buttermilk to dry ingredients. Mix well. Pour batter into cake pan.

- Bake 30-35 minutes. Remove from oven.

- Squeeze oranges. Add ¼ cup sugar to juice. Slowly pour over hot cake.

Yields 9 servings.

Upside Down Chocolate Mango Cake

Cake

- 1 medium mango, sliced
- ¼ cup light brown sugar
- 2 tablespoons butter
- ¾ cup flour
- ¾ cup sugar
- ⅓ cup unsweetened cocoa powder
- 1 teaspoon baking soda
- ¼ teaspoon salt
- ¾ cup buttermilk
- ¼ cup vegetable oil
- 1 large egg
- 3 tablespoons finely chopped candied ginger
- 1 teaspoon vanilla
  Topping
  nuts

- Set oven rack in lower third of oven. Preheat oven to 350°. Place drip pan or cookie sheet on oven floor to catch any drips.

- In saucepan, combine brown sugar and butter. Stir over medium heat until mixture is bubbling. Immediately pour it into 8x8-inch baking pan and spread mixture over bottom of pan. Arrange mango slices in spiral on top.

- Sift together flour, sugar, cocoa, baking soda and salt.

- Add buttermilk, oil, egg, candied ginger and vanilla.

- With electric mixer, beat batter on low speed just until combined. Increase speed to medium and beat 2 minutes.

- Pour batter over mango layer.

- Bake 35-40 minutes or until skewer inserted in center comes out clean.

- Run knife around edge of cake to loosen it. Invert onto serving plate. Brush topping over cake. Decorate edges with nuts.

- Serve warm or at room temperature.

Topping

- ¼ cup apricot or peach preserves, strained
- 1 tablespoon skinned and chopped pistachios or almonds

- In small saucepan, heat preserves until bubbling.

Yields 9 servings.

Poppy Seed Cake

Cake

2 cups sugar
1½ cups vegetable oil
4 eggs
1 teaspoon vanilla
3 cups flour
1½ teaspoons soda
1 teaspoon salt
1 13-ounce can evaporated milk or 8-ounce bottle whipping cream plus enough fresh milk to equal 13 ounces
½ 2.6-ounce bottle poppy seeds
1 cup chopped walnuts
Lemon Icing

- Preheat oven to 325°. Grease and flour bundt or tube pan.
- Beat sugar, oil and eggs until fluffy. Add vanilla and beat.
- Sift flour, soda and salt. Add flour mixture alternately with milk. Add poppy seeds and chopped nuts.
- Place in prepared pan.
- Bake 1 hour and 15 minutes.
- Cool. Drizzle until cake is covered completely with icing.

Lemon Icing

3-4 tablespoons lemon juice
powdered sugar

- Mix lemon juice with enough powdered sugar to achieve right consistency to drizzle over cool cake.

Yields 15-20 servings.

Black Bottom Cupcakes

1½ cups flour, unsifted
1 cup sugar
¼ cup unsweetened cocoa powder
1 teaspoon baking soda
½ teaspoon salt
1 cup water
5 tablespoons vegetable oil
1 tablespoon cider vinegar
1 teaspoon vanilla
  Chocolate-Chip Filling
3 tablespoons chopped walnuts, optional

Chocolate-Chip Filling

1 8-ounce package cream cheese
1 egg
⅓ cup sugar
1 6-ounce package semi-sweet chocolate chips

- In large bowl, stir together flour, sugar, cocoa, baking soda and salt.

- In another container beat together water, oil, vinegar and vanilla. Gradually add to dry ingredients. Stir until well blended.

- Fill liners halfway with batter. Top each with 1 tablespoon of Chocolate-Chip Filling then top with ½ teaspoon walnuts.

- Bake 25 minutes.

- Beat together cream cheese, egg and sugar until smooth. Stir in chocolate chips.

Yields 18 cupcakes.

Pie Crust

This is the best pie crust around.

2 cups flour
1 teaspoon salt
¾ cup shortening
4 tablespoons water

- Sift flour and salt together
- Cut shortening into dry ingredients using pastry cutter until mixture looks like fine crumbs.
- Add water, one tablespoon at a time. Toss mixture with fork until it holds itself together.

Yields double 9-inch pie crust.

Custard Kiwi Pie

1 pound (4-5) firm, ripe kiwis; 2 kiwis, peeled and sliced for garnish
3 large eggs
1 cup sugar
3 tablespoons flour
1 teaspoon vanilla
½ cup whole milk
1 graham cracker pie crust, pre-baked
powdered sugar for garnish

- Place rack in lower third of oven. Preheat oven to 375°.
- Peel kiwis, cut out core and slice in quarter-inch rounds.
- In large bowl, whisk eggs and sugar until combined. Whisk in flour, vanilla and milk until smooth. Gently stir in kiwis.
- Pour custard into pie shell.
- Bake 30 minutes or until custard is set.
- Serve warm, chilled or at room temperature. Garnish with dusting of powdered sugar and kiwi slices, up to 2 hours before serving.

Yields 8 servings.

324 calories; 10 grams fat; 27% calories from fat; 205 mg. sodium

Key Lime Pie

1 8-inch graham cracker pie crust, pre-baked
1 14-ounce can sweetened condensed milk
½ cup fresh lime juice
2 egg yolks, beaten
1 tablespoon grated lime peel
green food coloring, if desired
whipped cream

- Beat condensed milk, lime juice, egg yolks, lime peel and food coloring together. Pour into graham cracker crust. Refrigerate until filling sets.
- Serve with whipped cream.

Yields 6 servings.

Never-Fail Pecan Pie

3 eggs
⅓ cup butter, melted
⅔ cup sugar, very level
1 cup dark corn syrup
1 dash salt
1 cup pecan halves
1 9-inch, deep-dish pastry shell, unbaked
whipped cream

- Preheat oven to 350°.
- Beat eggs, melted butter, sugar, corn syrup and salt. Fold in pecans. Pour mixture into pastry shell.
- Bake 50 minutes. Serve with whipped cream.

Yields 8 servings.

Tropical Custard Pie

This foolproof crust does not have to be rolled out, pre-baked or chilled.

Pie Shell

1½ cups all-purpose flour
½ teaspoon salt
2 teaspoons sugar
½ cup vegetable oil
2 tablespoons milk

- Preheat oven to 450°.

- Before making pie shell, scald milk for custard. Pour 2 cups milk into 4-cup or larger oven-proof glass measuring cup and microwave on high 5 minutes. (Or scald milk on stovetop.) Set aside to cool slightly.

- Combine flour, salt and sugar. Pour in oil and milk. Mix with fork until dough holds together.

- Pat dough into bottom and up sides of 9½-inch pie dish.

Custard

2 cups milk, scalded (see above)
⅝ cup sugar
5 large eggs (or 6 medium)
⅛ teaspoon salt
¾ teaspoon vanilla
grated nutmeg, preferably freshly-grated
fresh tropical fruit such as papaya or mango

- Mix sugar into scalded milk. In 1-quart bowl, gently beat eggs and salt. Pouring slowly at first, mix scalded milk into eggs. Stir in vanilla. Pour custard mixture into unbaked pie shell. Sprinkle surface with grated nutmeg.

- Place on cookie sheet in center of oven.

- Bake 10 minutes at 450°, then lower heat to 325°. Bake 25 minutes until knife inserted in center comes out clean. Cool nearly to room temperature.

- Refrigerate 1-2 hours before serving. Accompany with fresh tropical fruit.

Yields 8 servings.

Almond Cookies

1 cup shortening
1 cup sugar
2 teaspoons almond extract
1 egg, well beaten
¼ teaspoon salt
1 teaspoon baking soda
3 cups flour
  red coloring or almonds to
    garnish

- Preheat oven to 350°.
- Cream together shortening and sugar. Add almond extract and egg. Mix well.
- Sift together salt, baking soda and flour. Cut dry ingredients into shortening mixture. Knead until soft.
- Form into walnut-sized balls.
- Place on cookie sheet and flatten slightly with hand. Dot center with food coloring or place almond in center.
- Bake 10-15 minutes.

Yields 6 dozen cookies.

57 calories; 3 grams fat; 47% calories from fat; 27 mg. sodium

"Cool" Cookies

½ cup butter
½ cup milk
2 cups sugar
½ cup cocoa powder
3 cups uncooked oatmeal
½ cup peanut butter
2 teaspoons vanilla

- In saucepan, combine butter, milk, sugar and cocoa. Bring to boil.
- Boil 1 minute.
- Add oatmeal, peanut butter and vanilla to cocoa mixture. Mix well.
- Drop by spoonfuls onto cookie sheet and refrigerate.

Yields 2-3 dozen.

Coconut Macaroons

¾ cup flour
½ teaspoon baking powder
1⅓ cups sugar, divided
½ teaspoon salt
6 egg whites
½ teaspoon cream of tartar
½ teaspoon vanilla
½ teaspoon almond extract
1 cup moist coconut

- Preheat oven to 300°. Line muffin tins with paper liners.
- Sift flour, baking powder, 1 cup sugar and salt together.
- Beat egg whites until foamy. Add cream of tartar and continue to beat until stiff. Gradually fold in ⅓ cup sugar. Add vanilla and almond. Carefully fold in sifted ingredients and coconut.
- Fill muffin cups half full.
- Bake 40 minutes.

Yields 2 dozen.

Aunty Elsie's Chocolate Chip Cookies

2 cups butter, softened
1½ cups sugar
1½ cups brown sugar
4 eggs
2½ cups chopped walnuts or pecans
1 12-ounce package chocolate chips
2 teaspoons vanilla
½ cup plus 1 tablespoon hot water
4 cups cake flour
1 teaspoon baking soda
½ teaspoon salt

- Preheat oven to 350°.
- Cream butter and sugars. Gradually stir in eggs, walnuts, chocolate chips, vanilla and hot water. Mix ingredients thoroughly.
- Combine cake flour, baking soda and salt. Add to mixture.
- Roll 1 teaspoon of batter into a ball. Place on cookie sheet and space approximately 2 inches apart.
- Bake 15 minutes.

Yields 2 dozen cookies.

Macadamia Nut Cookies

1 cup butter, softened
1 cup sugar
1 cup brown sugar
2 eggs
2 cups flour
1 teaspoon baking powder
1 teaspoon baking soda
¼ teaspoon salt
1 teaspoon vanilla
3 cups rolled oats
⅓ cup chocolate chips
1 cup raisins
1½ cups macadamia nuts, coarsely chopped

- Preheat oven to 350°. Grease cookie sheets.
- Cream butter and sugars. Add eggs, one at a time. Beat well.
- Sift together flour, baking powder and salt. Add to butter mixture and mix well.
- Add vanilla, rolled oats, chocolate chips, raisins and chopped macadamia nuts. Blend well.
- Drop on cookie sheet with tablespoon and press down lightly.
- Bake 15-18 minutes. Cool on wire racks.

Yields 6 dozen cookies.

Ginger Cookies

1½ cups butter, softened
2 cups sugar
2 eggs, beaten
1 cup molasses
4½ cups bread flour
4 teaspoons baking soda
1 teaspoon salt
1 teaspoon cloves
2 teaspoons ginger
2 teaspoons cinnamon

- Preheat oven to 350°.
- Cream butter and sugar. Add eggs. Beat well. Add molasses.
- Sift together flour, baking soda, salt, cloves, ginger and cinnamon. Stir into batter.
- Refrigerate dough until firm enough to roll. Roll into balls (approximately 1 tablespoonful batter). Place on cookie sheet and flatten with fork. Dip fork in sugar or warm water to avoid sticking.
- Bake 7-9 minutes.

Yields 9-10 dozen cookies.

Macadamia Macaroons

1 cup unsalted macadamia
   nuts, 16 macadamia nuts
   for garnish
⅔ cup sugar
1 large egg white
¼ teaspoon almond extract
   pinch of salt
   powdered sugar, sifted, for
   dusting

- Preheat oven to 350°. Lightly butter cookie sheet.

- Place 1 cup macadamia nuts and granulated sugar in bowl of food processor and process until just finely ground.

- Add egg white, almond extract and salt and process until just combined.

- Roll mixture into 16 (1-inch) balls. Place 2 inches apart on prepared cookie sheet. Slightly flatten cookies and dust with powdered sugar. Gently press 1 whole macadamia nut into each cookie.

- Bake 10 minutes or until pale golden. Transfer to rack and cool completely.

Yields 16 cookies.

Note: Will keep about 4 days in airtight tin at room temperature.

Mrs. Arimoto's Macadamia Nut Cookies

3 cups butter, softened
3 cups powdered sugar
5½ cups flour
1 teaspoon vanilla
1½ cups chopped macadamia
   nuts

- Preheat oven to 350°. Grease cookie sheet.

- Cream butter with sugar. Add flour, vanilla and macadamia nuts.

- Use tablespoon to drop dough onto cookie sheet.

- Bake 10-12 minutes.

Yields 6 dozen cookies.

Crunchy Macadamia Nut Cookies

1 cup butter, softened
1 cup margarine
2 teaspoons vanilla
2 cups powdered sugar
3½ cups flour
2 cups cornflakes, semi-crushed
1 cup chopped macadamia nuts

- Preheat oven to 350°. Grease cookie sheets.

- Cream butter and margarine. Add vanilla and sugar. Mix until light and fluffy.

- Add flour, cornflakes and nuts.

- Drop by teaspoonfuls onto cookie sheet. Flatten slightly.

- Bake about 15 minutes.

Yields 10 dozen cookies.

58 calories; 4 grams fat; 58% calories from fat; 44 mg. sodium

Salty Nut Bars

1 16-ounce package salted peanuts
4 tablespoons butter
1 12-ounce package peanut butter chips
1 can sweetened condensed milk
½ 10-ounce package miniature marshmallows

- Butter 9x13-inch pan.

- Spread half of peanuts over bottom of pan.

- Melt butter and chips in microwave. (Start with 30 seconds. Be careful not to overheat.) Stir well until smooth.

- Add milk and marshmallows. Mix well. Spread over peanuts. Top with remaining peanuts. Let set 24 hours and cut into bars.

Yields 12-15 bars.

Persimmon Cookies

**2-3 very ripe persimmons,
yielding 1 cup pulp**
½ cup butter, softened
1 cup sugar
1 egg, beaten
2 cups flour
1 teaspoon baking soda
½ teaspoon cinnamon
½ teaspoon ground cloves
½ teaspoon nutmeg
1 cup chopped nuts
½ cup raisins

- Preheat oven to 350°. Grease cookie sheet.

- Peel persimmons, remove seeds and mash to prepare pulp.

- Cream butter and sugar. Add egg. Mix in persimmon pulp.

- Combine flour, baking soda, cinnamon, cloves and nutmeg. Add to persimmon mixture. Stir in nuts and raisins.

- Drop by tablespoonfuls on cookie sheet.

- Bake 12-15 minutes or until golden brown.

Yields 4-5 dozen cookies.

Note: To ripen persimmons, place in plastic bag with apple. Keep on counter 1-2 days.

Ultimate Cookies

1 cup butter, softened
1 cup brown sugar
1 cup sugar
3 eggs
1 teaspoon vanilla
2 cups flour
1 teaspoon baking soda
¼ teaspoon baking powder
2 cups oatmeal
2 cups flake cereal
¾ cup shredded coconut (or one small package)
¾ cup peanut butter or butterscotch chips
1½ cups chocolate chips
1½ cups chopped macadamia nuts

- Preheat oven to 350°.
- Beat butter, sugars, eggs and vanilla until fluffy.
- Mix together flour, baking soda and baking powder. Add to butter mixture. Stir in oatmeal, cereal, coconut, peanut butter or butterscotch chips, chocolate chips and nuts.
- Drop batter by tablespoonfuls onto cookie sheet. Flatten with fork.
- Bake 8-10 minutes.

Yields 5 dozen.

Apricot Squares

¼ cup sugar
1⅓ cups flour, divided
1 teaspoon vanilla
½ cup butter, softened
⅔ cup dried California
  apricots
¼ cup water
2 eggs
1 cup brown sugar
½ teaspoon baking powder
1 cup chopped walnuts
  powdered sugar, optional

- Preheat oven to 350°.

- Combine sugar, 1 cup flour and vanilla. Cut butter into mixture until crumbly. Pat evenly into 8x8-inch pan. Bake 20 minutes.

- Cook apricots in water until soft. Drain and chop apricots.

- Beat eggs and brown sugar. Mix in apricots, ⅓ cup flour, baking powder and walnuts. Pour on baked crust.

- Bake 25-30 minutes until brown. Cool.

- If desired, sprinkle powdered sugar over top. Cut into 2-inch squares.

Yields 16 bars.

Substitute 1 cup granulated sugar plus 2 teaspoons molasses for 1 cup of brown sugar.

The Best Date Bars

Crust

½ **cup butter, softened**
¼ **cup sugar**
1 **cup sifted flour**

- Preheat oven to 400°.
- Mix butter, sugar and flour until crumbly. Press evenly in 9x9-inch or 7x11-inch pan.
- Bake 10-12 minutes. Do not brown crust.

Filling

⅓ **cup sifted flour**
½ **teaspoon baking powder**
¼ **teaspoon salt**
2 **eggs**
1 **cup brown sugar**
½ **cup chopped dates**
½ **cup walnut bits**
1 **teaspoon vanilla**

- Reduce oven to 350°.
- Mix together flour, baking powder and salt. Set aside.
- Beat eggs and add brown sugar and dates. Blend well. Add flour mixture, nuts and vanilla. Spread over baked crust.
- Bake 30 minutes or until set. Cut into squares while hot.

Yields 12-15 servings.

Energy Bars

3½ cups crispy rice cereal
2 cups rolled oats
⅓ cup sesame seeds
½ cup butter
½ cup peanut butter
1 10-ounce bag marshmallows (small ones melt faster)
1 cup unsalted peanuts, slightly chopped
1 cup raisins

- Place rice cereal, rolled oats, and sesame seeds in large pot and warm over very low heat for 5 minutes. Mix while heating.

- In separate large pan, over low heat, melt butter, peanut butter and marshmallows until blended.

- Add cereal mixture, peanuts and raisins to peanut butter mixture. Stir until well coated.

- Pour into 9x13-inch pan and press with spoon or fingers until flattened. Cool. Cut into bars and wrap individually in waxed paper.

Yields 39 3x1-inch servings.

129 calories; 7 grams fat; 45% calories from fat; 63 mg. sodium

Haupia Shortbread Bar

Crust

1 **cup butter**
2 **cups flour**
¼ **cup powdered sugar**

- Preheat oven to 350°.
- Cut butter into flour and powdered sugar. Press dough into 9x13-inch pan.
- Bake approximately 15-20 minutes or until crust is light brown. Cool.

Haupia (Coconut Pudding)

⅔ **cup sugar**
½ **cup cornstarch**
¼ **teaspoon salt**
1 **cup milk**
2 **12-ounce cans frozen coconut milk, defrosted**
1-2 **cups heavy cream, sweetened to taste and whipped**
flaked coconut for garnish

- Combine sugar, cornstarch and salt in pan. Slowly add milk, stirring to dissolve dry ingredients. Add defrosted coconut milk. Stir until smooth. Cook over medium heat until thickened. Boil 3 minutes, stirring constantly. Cool until lukewarm.
- Pour thickened mixture onto crust, spreading evenly. Chill.
- Top with whipped cream. Slice to desired size, then sprinkle with flaked coconut.

Yields 24 servings.

Note: To keep haupia from getting lumpy, stir occasionally while cooling. To speed up cooling, set pot in pan of cold water and keep pot covered with cloth to prevent top from drying.

Lemon Squares

6 tablespoons butter, softened
1⅔ cups sugar, divided
2 large eggs
1½ teaspoons baking powder
¼ teaspoon salt
1½ cups flour
½ cup milk
5 tablespoons lemon juice, divided

- Preheat oven to 350°. Grease and flour 13x9 inch pan.
- Cream butter and 1 cup sugar. Add eggs.
- Sift together baking powder, salt and flour. Add, alternately with milk, to creamed butter mixture. Add 3 tablespoons lemon juice. Pour batter into prepared pan.
- Bake 25 minutes.
- Combine ⅔ cup sugar and 2 tablespoons of lemon juice. While lemon squares are still warm, drizzle sugar-lemon mixture over top and return to oven 5 more minutes. Cut into squares and serve.

Yields 15 servings.

Fiendish Brownies

2 cups sugar
4 large eggs, beaten
⅛ teaspoon salt
½ cup butter, softened
4 ounces semi-sweet
    chocolate, melted
1 teaspoon vanilla
1 cup flour
¾ cup coarsely chopped
    nuts

- Preheat oven to 350°. Grease and flour 9x13-inch baking pan.

- Combine sugar, beaten eggs, salt and butter. Beat until smooth.

- Melt chocolate over hot water, let cool slightly and stir into egg mixture. Add vanilla. Beat until smooth.

- Mix in flour. Fold in nuts. Pour into prepared baking pan.

- Bake about 25 minutes or until cake tester inserted in middle comes out clean. Cool and cut into squares.

Yields 16-20 pieces.

Six squares (6 ounces) of semi-sweet chocolate equals one 6-ounce package semi-sweet chocolate pieces, or 6 tablespoons unsweetened cocoa powder plus ¼ cup sugar and ¼ cup shortening.

Pineapple Squares

½ cup butter, softened
1 cup sugar
4 eggs
1½ cups flour
1 teaspoon baking powder
½ teaspoon baking soda
¼ teaspoon salt
1 20-ounce can crushed
   pineapple, drained
   powdered sugar for
   garnish

- Preheat oven to 350°. Grease 9x13-inch pan.
- Cream butter and sugar. Add eggs and mix well.
- Combine flour, baking powder, baking soda and salt. Add to butter mixture. Add pineapple and stir until blended. Pour batter into pan.
- Bake 30-35 minutes.
- Cool and cut into bars. Sprinkle with powdered sugar.

Yields 24 servings.

121 calories; 5 grams fat; 35% calories from fat; 121 mg. sodium

Pineapple Nut Torte

1½ cups flour
¼ teaspoon salt
1 teaspoon baking powder
¼ teaspoon baking soda
3 eggs
1½ cups sugar
1 cup chopped walnuts
1½ cups drained, crushed
   pineapple
1 pint heavy cream,
   sweetened with sugar,
   whipped

- Preheat oven to 350°. Lightly grease two 9-inch round cake pans.
- Sift together flour, salt, baking powder and baking soda.
- Beat eggs and mix in sugar. Fold in walnuts and pineapple. Add sifted dry ingredients.
- Spread mixture, about 1-inch thick, in prepared pans.
- Bake 40-50 minutes.
- Serve hot or cold with whipped cream.

Yields 15 servings.

Mango Bars

Crust

- 1 cup butter
- 2 cups flour
- 2 tablespoons powdered sugar

- Preheat oven to 350°. Oil 9x13-inch pan.
- Cut butter in flour and powdered sugar to pea size and pat into pan. Bake for 10-15 minutes.

Filling

- 4 cups chopped mangoes
- ¾ cup sugar
- ⅓ cup water
- 3 tablespoons cornstarch
  water to dilute cornstarch

- Combine mangoes, sugar and water. Cook until soft. Add cornstarch mixed with water and cook until clear. Cool slightly and pour filling over crust.

Topping

- ½ cup butter
- 2 cups oatmeal
- ½ cup sugar
- ¼ cup flour

- Cut butter in oatmeal, sugar, and flour mixture to pea size and sprinkle evenly over filling. Bake for about 50 minutes.

Yields 25-30 pieces.

Mochi

Japanese rice flour (mochiko) is the basis for a variety of delicious desserts called mochi.

- 1 16-ounce box mochiko
- ¼ teaspoon baking powder
- 2½ cups sugar
- 2 cups water
- 1 13.5-ounce can coconut milk
- ¼ teaspoon red coloring
  cornstarch or kinako
  (soybean flour)

- Preheat oven to 350°. Grease 9x13-inch pan.
- Mix all ingredients together. Pour mixture into pan. Cover with foil.
- Bake 1 hour. Cool. Store in covered container.
- Next day, cut and roll in cornstarch or kinako.

Yields 28 servings.

Apricot Mochi

1 16-ounce box mochiko
(3½ cups)
2 3-ounce boxes apricot-
flavored gelatin
1½ cups sugar
1 12-ounce can apricot
nectar
1½ cups water
potato starch or kinako
(soy bean flour)

- Preheat oven to 350°. Grease 9x13-inch pan.
- Combine all ingredients except potato starch or kinako. Mix well. Pour into baking pan. Cover tightly with aluminum foil.
- Bake 55-60 minutes.
- Remove from oven; after 15 minutes, remove foil. Cool for several hours.
- Cool and cut with plastic knife. Roll in potato starch or kinako. Shake off excess starch. Store in covered container.

Yields 28 servings.

Variation: Substitute peach for apricot-flavored gelatin. Vary flavor with different juice and gelatin combinations such as strawberry or cherry.

Custard Poi Mochi

1 cup butter, melted
4 cups mochiko
1 12-ounce can evaporated
milk
1 tablespoon baking powder
2 cups sugar
4 eggs
1 pound fresh poi, undiluted

- Preheat oven to 350°. Grease and flour 9x13-inch pan.
- Mix all ingredients and pour into pan.
- Bake 1 hour.
- Cool and cut with plastic knife. Store in covered container.

Yields 40 pieces.

Aunty Bessie's Butter Mochi

6 tablespoons butter, softened
2¼ cups sugar
4 eggs
1 16-ounce box mochiko
2 teaspoons baking powder
1 teaspoon vanilla
1 12-ounce can evaporated milk plus enough water to make 2 cups liquid
1 13.5-ounce can coconut milk

- Preheat oven to 350°. Lightly grease 9x13-inch pan.
- Cream butter and sugar together. Add eggs, mochiko, baking powder, vanilla, evaporated milk and coconut milk. Stir well. Pour into pan.
- Bake 1 hour.
- Cool and cut with plastic knife. Store in covered container.

Yields 28 servings.

Pumpkin Mochi

A delightful version of a pumpkin dessert.

4 eggs, beaten
2 cups sugar
1 29-ounce can pumpkin purée
1 14-ounce can condensed milk
1 cup butter, melted and cooled
2 teaspoons vanilla
1 16-ounce box plus ¼ cup mochiko (3¾ cups)
2 teaspoons baking powder
1½ teaspoons pumpkin spice (or ½ teaspoon each of ginger, nutmeg and ground cloves)
½ teaspoon cinnamon

- Preheat oven to 350°. Lightly grease 9x13-inch pan.
- Mix together eggs, sugar, pumpkin, milk, butter and vanilla.
- Sift together mochiko, baking powder, pumpkin spices and cinnamon. Add to pumpkin mixture. Beat until smooth.
- Place in prepared pan and smooth surface.
- Bake 1 hour.
- Cool completely. Cut with plastic knife. Store in covered container.

Yields 28 servings.

Applejack Cobbler

Great on buffet table as it is delicious served at room temperature.

Apple Mixture

**8 cups thinly-sliced, peeled
apples (about 5 Rome
Beauties or Granny
Smiths)**
½ cup dried currants
½ cup chopped dates
½ cup golden raisins
**½ cup applejack, apple juice
or apple cider**

- Preheat oven to 350°. Lightly coat 7x10-inch baking pan with nonstick cooking spray.
- Spread apple slices on bottom of pan. Sprinkle with dried fruits. Pour applejack over mixture.

Batter topping

2 cups flour
½ cup sugar
2 teaspoons baking powder
½ teaspoon salt (optional)
1 teaspoon cinnamon
⅛ teaspoon nutmeg
**⅓ cup butter, slightly
softened**
1 cup skim milk
**1 cup apple cider or juice,
heated to boiling**

- Combine flour, sugar, baking powder, salt, cinnamon and nutmeg in large bowl. Cut in butter until mixture is grainy. Just before baking, stir in milk. (Food processor will make topping more fluid and easier to distribute over fruit mixture.)
- Spoon batter topping over fruit.
- Gently pour hot cider or apple juice over topping.
- Bake about 25 minutes, until most of juice has been absorbed.

Yields 12 servings.

276 calories; 6 fat grams; 18% calories from fat; 147 mg. sodium

Banana Tapioca

10 medium ripe apple
    bananas or 5 regular
    bananas
1¼ cups sugar, divided
 ½ cup tapioca
 1 10-ounce can coconut
    milk
 2 cups warm water,
    additional water to soak
    tapioca
    dash salt
 ½ cup unsalted peanuts,
    coarsely ground

- Peel and cut bananas in 1-inch lengths, diagonally.
- In large bowl, sprinkle ¼ cup sugar evenly on bananas. Let stand about 15 minutes.
- Meantime, soak tapioca 10 minutes in water. Drain water off.
- Add coconut milk and 1 cup water to banana mixture.
- Cook 20 minutes on medium heat. Add remaining sugar and 1 cup water. Bring to boil and add tapioca.
- Cook 15 minutes or until tapioca is clear. Add salt.
- Sprinkle peanuts on tapioca just before serving. Can be served hot or cold.

Yields 10 servings.

To freeze overripe bananas, toss unpeeled fruit into plastic bag and freeze. When ready to use, thaw about 1 hour. Drain excess water, peel and mash.

Broiled Bananas and Pineapple

1 large ripe banana
4 slices fresh or drained
   canned pineapple
2 tablespoons firmly packed
   brown sugar
1 tablespoon butter
   sour cream or plain
   yogurt

- Preheat broiler.

- Peel banana. Cut in half crosswise, then cut each piece in half lengthwise.

- Arrange banana pieces and pineapple slices in single layer in 9- or 10-inch pan. Sprinkle with sugar and dot with butter.

- Broil about 6 inches below heat until fruit is glazed (about 6 minutes), basting a few times.

- Spoon hot fruit into 2 dessert dishes and top each serving with sour cream. Pour any remaining hot butter sauce from pan over sour cream.

Yields 2 servings.

Tropical Bananas

1 cup dry white wine
2 4-inch cinnamon sticks
1 cup firmly packed dark
  brown sugar
12 cloves
½ cup pineapple juice
  pinch of freshly grated
    nutmeg
6 firm bananas, halved
    lengthwise and crosswise
  ice cream

- In saucepan, combine the wine, cinnamon sticks, brown sugar, cloves, pineapple juice and nutmeg.

- Boil 5 minutes until mixture thickens slightly.

- Add banana halves.

- Simmer 5 minutes, turning the bananas once.

- Place scoop of ice cream in serving bowl. Spoon bananas and sauce over it.

Yields 6 servings.

Variation: Whip cream and season with nutmeg, almond extract and sugar to taste. Place bananas on serving platter and serve with whipped cream on side.

285 calories; 1 fat gram; 2% calories from fat; 18 mg. sodium

Pineapple Bread Pudding

This "comfort food" is moist, delicious and lower in fat than traditional bread puddings.

6 slices white or whole wheat bread, toasted and cut into cubes, crusts removed
¼ cup chopped dates
¼ cup currants or raisins (optional: soak in ¼ cup warm rum for 5 minutes or in the liquid drained from crushed pineapple; drain)
1 cup canned crushed pineapple, drained
1 whole egg
2 egg whites
½ cup sugar, 1 tablespoon sugar
⅓ cup water
1 teaspoon vanilla
½ teaspoon grated nutmeg
½ teaspoon cinnamon, 1 tablespoon cinnamon
1 13-ounce can evaporated skim milk

- Preheat oven to 350°. Spray 8x8-inch pan with nonstick cooking spray.
- Place half of bread cubes on bottom of baking pan. Sprinkle with dates and raisins. Spread with crushed pineapple. Top with remaining bread cubes.
- Beat egg and egg whites with ½ cup sugar until frothy. Add water, vanilla, nutmeg, ½ teaspoon cinnamon and evaporated milk. Beat until well mixed.
- Pour egg mixture over bread. Sprinkle 1 tablespoon sugar and 1 tablespoon cinnamon on top.
- Bake 40 minutes, until toothpick placed in the center comes out clean.
- Cool and cut into squares.

Yields 12 servings.

Note: Can be made a day ahead. For buffet, cut into smaller pieces and place in colorful paper cups.

Bavarian Tart

Bottom Crust

2 cups flour
1 cup butter
**2 heaping tablespoons
   powdered sugar**

- Preheat oven to 350°. Grease 9x13-inch pan.
- Cut butter into flour and powdered sugar and press mixture in pan.
- Bake 15 minutes or until crust is lightly browned.
- Take pan out of oven and set aside. Leave oven on.

Filling

**2 8-ounce packages cream
   cheese**
½ cup sugar
2 eggs
1 teaspoon vanilla

- Beat cream cheese. Add sugar and continue to beat. Add eggs and vanilla and beat until mixture is creamy and fluffy. Pour mixture on crust.

Topping

**2 29-ounce cans pears
   dash of cinnamon**

- Drain and cut pears in wedges and place them evenly on cream cheese filling. Sprinkle cinnamon over top.
- Bake 50-60 minutes.

Yields 24-30 servings.

English Trifle

1 sponge cake or angel food
  cake
  raspberry jam
3 eggs
3 teaspoons sugar
10 ounces milk
½ cup cream sherry
½ pint whipping cream
  glacé cherries, chopped
    walnuts or fruit for
    topping

- Cut cake in half horizontally. Spread freshly cut side of each with raspberry jam. Cut into 2-inch squares.

- To make custard, beat eggs slightly, then add sugar. Heat milk until just before boiling. Pour over eggs and sugar. Return mixture to low heat. Cook slowly, stirring until thick. Do not boil. Cool.

- In pretty glass bowl, assemble trifle in 3 layers: cake, sherry and custard. Repeat twice.

- Chill at least 1 hour or overnight.

- Before serving, whip cream and spoon over trifle. Decorate with cherries, nuts or fruit such as raspberries or strawberries.

Yields 8 servings.

Variation: Add fresh fruit such as berries or canned fruit such as sliced peaches to each layer as trifle is assembled.

Note: Jelly rolls have a more authentic cake texture. If using jelly roll, unroll and scrape off jelly. Proceed with recipe.

Pear Kuchen

½ **cup butter, softened**
½ **cup sugar**
3 **eggs**
½ **teaspoon almond extract**
1 **cup flour**
⅓ **cup nuts, finely ground**
3 **large, ripe pears**
   powdered sugar

- Preheat oven to 350°. Butter and flour 11-inch tart pan (removable bottom).

- Cream butter and sugar. Beat in eggs one at a time until fluffy. Stir in almond extract. Fold in flour and nuts.

- Spoon batter into tart pan and spread evenly.

- Peel and slice pears. Arrange decoratively on batter, pressing gently.

- Bake until crust is firm to touch, about 40 minutes. Cool and dust with powdered sugar.

Yields 12 servings.

Pavlova

Light-as-air meringue dessert from Downunder named after Russian ballerina Anna Pavlova.

3 egg whites
3 tablespoons cold water
1 cup sugar
¼ teaspoon salt
1 tablespoon cornstarch
1 teaspoon vanilla
1 teaspoon vinegar
  whipped cream, sweetened to taste with sugar and vanilla
  fresh kiwis and strawberries (or freshest, most appealing fruit available)

- Preheat oven to 350°. Cover cookie sheet with waxed paper and grease paper.

- Beat egg whites until very stiff. Add water and beat again. Add sugar, 1 tablespoon at a time, beating until thick and glossy.

- Fold in salt, cornstarch, vanilla and vinegar.

- Mound onto cookie sheet and spread to size of dinner plate.

- Bake 15 minutes. Turn oven off and leave meringue in oven for at least one hour. Outside should be crisp shell, inside almost a marshmallow texture.

- To serve, turn meringue upside down onto serving plate and spread with layer of whipped cream. Arrange fresh fruit attractively on top.

Yields 6-8 servings.

147 calories; 0 grams fat; 0 calories from fat; 126 mg. sodium (shells only-not including whipped cream and fruit)

Gingersnap and Bourbon Truffles

8 ounces semisweet chocolate, chopped
½ cup unsalted butter
⅔ cup finely crushed gingersnaps
3 tablespoons bourbon
⅓ cup unsweetened cocoa powder
⅓ cup powdered sugar

- In heavy pan, melt chocolate and butter over low heat, stirring until smooth. Add cookies and bourbon.

- Transfer to bowl and refrigerate about 45 minutes or until firm.

- Line cookie sheet with foil. Using a teaspoon, drop truffle mixture onto cookie sheet.

- Freeze 15 minutes.

- With your hands, roll each truffle into smooth round ball.

- Sift cocoa and powdered sugar into shallow bowl. Roll each truffle in powder.

- Store up to 1 week in refrigerator in covered air-tight tin.

- Before serving, remove from refrigerator and let stand at room temperature.

Yields 24 truffles.

Fifteen gingersnaps equals 1 cup finely crushed gingersnap crumbs.

Super Chocolate Sauce for Ice Cream

1½ cups sugar
½ cup cocoa powder
   (preferably Dutch
   processed)
3 tablespoons cornstarch
2½ tablespoons butter
¼ teaspoon salt
1 cup boiling water

- In saucepan, mix together sugar, cocoa and cornstarch.
- Add butter, salt and water. Bring to boiling point.
- Reduce heat to low and cook 4 minutes, stirring constantly. Serve hot or cold.

Yields 16 (2 tablespoon) servings.

105 calories; 2 fat grams; 17% calories from fat; 56 mg. sodium

Brandy-Wine Fruit Sauce

½ cup brandy
½ cup red wine
1 cup whole cranberry sauce
½ 6-ounce can frozen orange
   juice, undiluted
½ lemon, peel removed from
   half of it
   fresh strawberries, kiwis,
   grapes and bananas, cut
   into bite-size pieces

- Place brandy, wine, cranberry sauce, orange juice, and lemon in blender. Process until smooth. Strain. Refrigerate until ready to use.
- Spoon fresh fruit into champagne glasses. Ladle spoonful of sauce over fruit or, several hours before serving, marinate fruit in sauce.

Yields sauce for 12-15 servings.

70 calories; 0 fat grams; 0% calories from fat; 6 mg. sodium

Lime Cheesecake

favorite graham cracker or shortbread crust

1 3-ounce package lime gelatin

⅔ cup hot water

1 8-ounce package cream cheese

½ cup sugar, 2 tablespoons sugar

¼ teaspoon vanilla

¼ teaspoon lemon extract

1 cup heavy cream

- Prepare favorite crust. Cover and chill.

- Dissolve gelatin in hot water. When cool, refrigerate until syrupy, about 30-45 minutes. Then beat until frothy and set aside.

- Beat cream cheese with ½ cup sugar until fluffy. Add vanilla and lemon extract. Combine with gelatin mixture.

- Whip cream until thick. Add 2 tablespoons sugar and fold into lime-cream-cheese mixture. Pour into crust and chill until set.

Yields 8 servings.

CELEBRITY CHEFS

Celebrity Chefs' Recipes

Hawaii's chefs have earned national and international acclaim for combining local and international ingredients and cooking styles, especially from the Pacific Rim.

We are very grateful for their contributions to this cookbook.

Rillettes of Two Salmon Served on Waimanalo Greens

Chef Jean-Luc Voegele, Bali-by-the-Sea, Hilton Hawaiian Village

1½ **pounds fresh salmon filet**
3 **quarts court bouillon (stock)**
½ **cup salted butter, softened**
1 **egg yolk**
 lemon juice
3 **tablespoons extra virgin olive oil**
 dash Tabasco sauce
 salt and pepper, to taste
½ **ounce chopped green onion**
½ **ounce dill**
4½ **ounces smoked salmon (cubed)**
4 **ounces Waimanalo greens**
2 **ounces Balsamic Dressing**
6 **slices toasted French bread**

- Poach salmon in court bouillon 10 minutes. Remove and cool.
- Place butter in mixing bowl and whip 2 minutes.
- Add egg yolk, lemon juice, oil, Tabasco, salt, pepper, onion, dill and smoked salmon.
- Flake poached salmon. Add to smoked salmon mixture and mix well.
- Using a soup spoon, take 1 scoop of salmon mixture, and, placing a second soup spoon over the mixture, create a quenelle.
- Toss greens with dressing and arrange on plate with salmon rillette quenelles.
- Serve with warm, toasted French bread on side.

Balsamic Dressing

⅓ **cup balsamic vinegar**
⅔ **cup extra virgin olive oil**
1 **teaspoon Dijon mustard**
1 **tablespoon chopped shallots**
 salt and pepper, to taste

- Whisk all ingredients together.

Yields 6 servings.

Lobster Curry with Haupia

Chef Steve Chiang, Golden Dragon Restaurant,
Hilton Hawaiian Village

1 **ounce green peas**
1 **ounce carrots**
 oil for deep frying
2 **ounces cubed potatoes**
2 **tablespoons vegetable oil**
1 **ounce chopped onion**
8 **ounces lobster tails, cut**
 into chunks
1 **ounce curry powder**
2 **ounces coconut milk**
1 **ounce half and half**
2 **ounces chicken stock**
 Thickening Sauce
1 **ounce raisins**
 salt and pepper, to taste

- Bring pot of water to boil. Blanch green peas and carrots. Drain well and set aside.
- Deep fry potato cubes for 2 minutes until cooked; set aside.
- Heat wok. Add 2 tablespoons vegetable oil and, when hot, reduce heat slightly.
- Stir-fry onion and lobster 2 minutes until cooked thoroughly.
- Add curry powder, coconut milk, half and half and chicken stock. Stir-fry 1 minute longer.
- Stir in Thickening Sauce and add peas, carrots, potatoes and raisins. Season with salt and pepper. Bring to boil. Transfer to serving dish with deep-fried haupia on side for garnish.

Thickening Sauce

2 **tablespoons cornstarch**
2 **tablespoons chicken stock**

- Combine cornstarch and chicken stock.

(Continued)

(Lobster Curry with Haupia, continued)

Haupia

1½ cups coconut milk
⅓ cup sugar
¾ cup water
5 tablespoons cornstarch

- Heat coconut milk and sugar in double boiler. Mix water and cornstarch together. Stir into coconut milk until smooth.

- Cook and stir mixture over low heat until it thickens completely. Increase heat slightly and stir mixture vigorously to prevent it from burning.

- When coconut milk fat begins to melt, mixture is done. It will be sticky. Remove mixture from stove and pour into 9x8-inch cake pan; let cool until set.

Dusting

2 tablespoons cornstarch
vegetable oil

- Cut Haupia into 2-inch diamond-shaped cubes and dust with cornstarch. Deep fry in vegetable oil for 2 minutes.

Yields 2-4 servings.

Ahi Poke Dip

Chef Oliver Altherr, Hoku's, Kahala Mandarin Oriental

2 cups mayonnaise
½ cup gari shoga (pickled ginger)
½ cup chopped green onion
½ cup chopped cilantro
¼ cup toasted sesame seeds
½ cup lemon juice
½ cup soy sauce
2 teaspoons white pepper
¾ cup diced fresh ahi

- Mix all ingredients together. Keep chilled until ready to serve. If preparing ahead, mix all but pepper and ahi together.

- Mixture can be stored in refrigerator up to a week. Fold in pepper and ahi just before serving.

Yields 5 cups.

Island Tropical Poke

Chef Sam Choy, Sam Choy's Restaurants

3 pounds fresh fish, such as ahi or aku, cubed
sea salt, to taste
2 finely chopped chili peppers (seeds removed)
¾ cup diced tomato
¾ cup chopped ogo (fresh seaweed)
¾ cup diced onions
¾ cup chopped green onion
1 fresh green half-ripe mango, diced
¾ cup soy sauce
1 tablespoon sesame seed oil
½ cup coconut milk

- Cube fresh fish and add salt, chili peppers, tomato, ogo and onions. Toss lightly.
- Add mango, soy sauce and oil and toss lightly.
- Add coconut milk and toss lightly.

Yields 6-12 servings.

Lanai Pineapple Gazpacho

Chef Edwin Goto, The Lodge at Koele

1 cup peeled, seeded and coarsely chopped cucumber
¼ cup coarsely chopped red bell pepper
¼ cup coarsely chopped yellow bell pepper
1 teaspoon finely minced jalapeño pepper
⅛ cup coarsely chopped Maui onion
1 cup coarsely chopped fresh pineapple
1 tablespoon coarsely chopped Italian parsley
½ cup pineapple cider or pineapple juice
pinch of salt

- Place chopped ingredients in blender with pineapple cider and salt. Blend until mixture is smooth.
- Chill and serve.

Yields 2-4 servings.

96 calories; 1 gram fat; 5% calories from fat; 5 mg. sodium

Kahala Caesar Salad

Chef Kelvin Ro, Kahala Moon Cafe

1 teaspoon minced garlic
1 teaspoon minced shallot
2 tablespoons olive oil, 15
ounces olive oil
1 teaspoon minced
anchovies
4 ounces rice wine vinegar
1 ounce sherry vinegar
salt and pepper, to taste
8 ounces cleaned and
trimmed romaine hearts
2 ounces shredded
Parmesan cheese
1 teaspoon chopped,
toasted macadamia nuts

- Toast garlic and shallots with just enough olive oil to cover in small sauce pot. Cool.

- To prepare the vinaigrette, place garlic, shallots and anchovies in medium bowl. Add rice wine vinegar, sherry vinegar and oil in steady stream, whisking constantly. Season with salt and pepper.

- Toss romaine hearts with 1 ounce vinaigrette.

- Garnish with shredded Parmesan cheese and macadamia nuts.

Yields 1 serving salad,
2½ cups dressing.

Kalua Duck Quesadillas

Chef David Paul Johnson, David Paul's Diamond Head Grill

Kalua Duck

- **4 duck legs, including thighs**
- **1 tablespoon kosher salt**
- **1 tablespoon black pepper, ground and toasted**
- **1 quart rendered duck fat or light vegetable oil**
- **1 ounce liquid smoke**
- **2 cloves garlic, peeled**
- **½ ounce black peppercorns**

- Preheat oven to 275°.
- Preheat grill.
- Season duck legs with salt and pepper. Grill until golden brown.
- Heat duck fat or oil in flame-proof baking dish to 275°. Add liquid smoke and pour over duck pieces. Add garlic and peppercorns. Make sure duck legs are completely covered with fat. Cover with foil.
- Bake 3 hours.
- Remove and cool to room temperature. Store duck in fat, in refrigerator, until ready to use.

Avocado Relish

- **1 ripe avocado**
- **2 tablespoons finely diced Maui onion**
- **1 tablespoon chopped fresh cilantro**
- **½ tablespoon sour cream salt and pepper, to taste**
- **1 teaspoon lime juice**

- Peel, seed and cut avocado into medium dice.
- Gently fold in onions, cilantro and sour cream. Salt and pepper to taste. Stir in lime juice. Keep covered and refrigerated until ready to use.

Yields approximately 1½ cups.

(Continued)

(Kalua Duck Quesadillas, continued)

Pico de Gallo

1 **small-medium tomato, diced and drained**
2 **tablespoons diced onion**
1 **tablespoon chopped fresh cilantro**
1 **teaspoon chopped garlic**
½ **teaspoon diced green jalapeño**
  salt and pepper, to taste

Chipotle Aioli

1 **extra large egg yolk**
½ **teaspoon minced garlic**
5 **ounces vegetable oil**
½ **ounce apple cider vinegar**
  salt and white pepper, to taste
⅓ **ounce canned chipotle peppers, seeded and diced**

Assembling the Quesadillas

8 **8-inch flour tortillas**
12 **ounces Kalua duck, shredded**
1 **12-ounce package Monterey Jack cheese, shredded**
4 **tablespoons Avocado Relish**
4 **tablespoons Pico de Gallo**
4 **teaspoons Chipotle Aioli cilantro leaves**

- Combine all ingredients and season to taste. Let stand at least 1 hour to develop flavors.

Yields 1 cup.

- Process egg and garlic in food processor. Add oil very slowly, then in a steady stream once emulsification has been formed. Thin with vinegar as needed and, if more thinning is needed, with water.

- Season with salt, white pepper, chipotle peppers and some liquid from can of peppers. This adds spicy and smoky flavor.

Yields 1 cup.

- Lightly oil skillet.
- Cover slightly less than ½ of tortilla with ⅛ cheese and ⅛ shredded duck. Fold remaining half over filling. Place in skillet and cook to a golden brown on both sides. Repeat with remaining tortillas.

- Cut each quesadilla into thirds and arrange six pieces on each of 4 serving plates.

- Top each serving with 1 tablespoon Avocado Relish, 1 tablespoon Pico de Gallo and 1 teaspoon Chipotle Aioli. Garnish with cilantro leaves.

Yields 4 servings plus extra sauce.

Grilled Portabello Tower with Vine-Ripened Organic Tomatoes and Balsamic Vinaigrette

Chef Jean-Marie Josselin, A Pacific Cafe

Portabello Tower

1 **cup extra virgin olive oil**
2 **tablespoons chopped basil**
1 **teaspoon minced garlic**
2 **red vine-ripened tomatoes**
2 **yellow vine-ripened tomatoes**
  pinch salt and pepper
1 **large eggplant**
4 **portabello mushrooms**

- Mix oil, basil and minced garlic together to form marinade. Cut each tomato into four slices. Pour ½ of marinade over tomatoes, season with salt and pepper and marinate at room temperature for 30 minutes.

- Slice eggplant into 8 rings (similar to tomato slices). Marinate eggplant and portabello with rest of marinade for 30 minutes. Season with salt and pepper.

- Preheat broiler.

- Place eggplant on oven pan and broil 5-7 minutes until done. Broil portabello the same way, until mushroom is soft. Remove both mushroom and eggplant from oven and allow to cool.

Balsamic Vinaigrette

1 **clove minced garlic**
4 **leaves basil, chopped**
1 **tablespoon honey**
½ **teaspoon Dijon mustard**
2 **cloves shallots, minced**
½ **cup balsamic vinaigrette**
1½ **cups olive oil**
  salt and pepper, to taste

- Whisk all ingredients together except oil. Whisking quickly, add oil slowly, until oil is incorporated.

(Continued)

(Grilled Portabello Tower with Vine-Ripened Organic Tomatoes and Balsamic Vinaigrette, continued)

Basil Pesto

1 small clove garlic
1 cup fresh basil
¾ cup olive oil
 salt and pepper, to taste

- Process all ingredients together in blender until consistency is smooth.

Assembling Portabello Tower

Balsamic Vinaigrette
portabello
tomatoes
eggplant
basil tops
thyme sprig
Basil Pesto

- Place Balsamic Vinaigrette in center of plate to form 4-inch diameter circle.
- Place portabello and then alternate red tomato, yellow tomato and eggplant until two slices of each makes up tower.
- Top with basil and thyme. This will give dish some height. Drizzle Basil Pesto around Balsamic Vinaigrette.

Yields 4 servings.

Ti Leaf Steamed Seafood

Chef Russell Siu, 3660 On-the-Rise

8 **large ti leaves, cleaned**
2 **bunches spinach, cleaned
  and stemmed**
1 **cup basil, destemmed,
  loosely packed**
12 **ounces opakapaka cut
  into 1-inch squares**
  salt and pepper, to taste
12 **pieces shrimp, 21-25
  count, peeled and
  deveined**
20 **scallops**
4 **large Roma tomatoes,
  diced**
1½ **cups sliced button
  mushrooms**
  **Lemon Tomato Butter
  Sauce**
  green onions, finely cut

- On large work area, place 2 ti leaves in "t" pattern. Repeat with remaining 3 pairs.

- Toss together spinach and basil. Divide into 8 portions. Place 1 portion of spinach into center of each t-shaped pattern.

- In large bowl, toss fish with salt and pepper to taste.

- Place equal amounts of fish on top of spinach.

- Toss shrimp and scallops in separate bowls with salt and pepper.

- In center of fish, place 3 shrimp and 5 scallops.

- Top with 1 diced tomato and ¼ of mushrooms.

- Use remaining spinach portion to cover seafood. Pick up the four ends and tie tightly with butcher's twine. Repeat with each grouping.

- Steam in steamer or double boiler approximately 20 minutes until done.

- Place ti leaf bundle in middle of plate. Cut strings and fold ends under bundle. Drizzle Lemon Tomato Butter Sauce over seafood and garnish with green onions.

(Continued)

(Ti Leaf Steamed Seafood, continued)

Lemon Tomato Butter Sauce

⅛ **cup diced green onion**

2 **small Roma tomatoes, seeded and diced**

2 **tablespoons finely diced red onion**

1 **tablespoon chopped shallots**

¼ **cup rice vinegar**

¼ **cup white wine**

¼ **cup heavy cream**

1 **cup butter cut into small pieces**
   juice of 1 lemon

- In small bowl, toss together green onion, tomatoes and red onion. Reserve.

- In separate saucepan combine shallots, rice vinegar and wine. Reduce by ½ and add cream. Reduce by ½ or until cream thickens. Reduce heat and add butter slowly, whisking constantly until smooth. Remove from heat and season with salt and pepper. Strain with fine sieve.

- Add reserved green onion mixture. Place in warm area of kitchen.

To serve: Place ti leaf bundle in middle of plate. Cut strings and fold stems under bundle. Drizzle sauce lightly over seafood and garnish with shaved onions.

Yields 8 servings.

Portuguese Bean Soup

Chef David St. Laurent, Morning Sous Chef, Hilton Hawaiian Village

2 pounds dried red kidney beans
8 ounces dried navy beans
2 gallons water
bacon trimmings
4 large ham hocks
1 cup vegetable oil
10 ounces diced celery
10 ounces diced onions
10 ounces diced carrots
4 ounces ham, diced
10 ounces diced Portuguese sausage
2 cloves garlic, finely chopped
1 cup tomato paste
2 gallons beef or ham stock
salt, pepper, chili powder, bay leaves, dash coriander powder
6 ounces diced potatoes
6 ounces diced cabbage
2 cups diced tomatoes

• Soak red kidney beans and navy beans overnight. Drain.

• Bring beans to boil with bacon trimmings and ham hocks. Simmer until beans are tender, 1½ to 2 hours. Cool overnight.

• Discard trimmings and debone ham hocks. Cut meat in cubes.

• Heat oil in large pan. Add celery, onions, carrots and sauté with ham, ham hocks (meat only, cubed), Portuguese sausage and garlic. Add tomato paste and fill up with stock.

• Drain beans and add to soup. Bring to boil.

• Add seasonings. Reduce heat and simmer for 1½ hours. Adjust seasonings. As soup simmers, skim excess oil off surface.

• Add potatoes, cabbage and tomatoes. Boil another 15-20 minutes.

Yields a large pot of hearty soup (5 gallons).

Kalua Duckling

Chef Gary Strehl, Hawaii Prince Hotel

2 duck legs, including
    thighs
2 teaspoons minced ginger
2 teaspoons minced garlic
1 cup chopped green onions
2 cups diced carrots and
    celery
2 cups sliced shiitake
    mushrooms
1 cup hoisin sauce
½ cup hot pepper sauce
    (Szechuan sauce
    available in Asian food
    market)
2 quarts duck or chicken
    stock
¾ teaspoon 5-spice powder
4 pieces star anise
1 cup Madeira wine
½ teaspoon chopped fresh
    thyme
cornstarch
cooked rice
stir-fried vegetables

- Season duck meat and brown well in very hot saucepan. No cooking oil will be necessary with high fat content of duck.

- Remove duck and using same pan, sauté ginger, garlic, green onions, carrots, celery and mushrooms until lightly browned.

- Place duck back into mushrooms and vegetables in pan and spoon hoisin and hot pepper sauce over duck, coating duck heavily.

- Add stock, 5-spice powder, star anise, wine and thyme. Simmer gently approximately 1½ hours. Legs should be cooked until meat is falling off bones.

- Remove duck from sauce and adjust thickness of sauce using small amount of cornstarch, if necessary.

- When meat has cooled, shred by hand and add back to sauce.

- Serve with rice and stir-fried vegetables.

Yields 2 servings.

Hibachi Tuna with Maui Onion Salad and Ponzu Sauce

Chef Roy Yamaguchi, Roy's Restaurant

Marinade

- **1 cup soy sauce**
- **1 tablespoon chopped garlic**
- **1 tablespoon minced ginger**
- **½ cup sliced scallions**
- **½ cup sugar**
- **4 ahi fillets, 7 ounces each**

- Combine marinade ingredients together in large mixing bowl. Marinate tuna for 1 hour.

- About 30 minutes before serving, get hibachi or barbecue grill ready and prepare salad.

Maui Onion Salad

- **1 large carrot, sliced**
- **1 small Maui onion, julienned**
- **4 ounces Japanese spice sprouts, tops only**
- **½ Japanese cucumber, seeded and julienned**
- **¼ cup pink pickled ginger**
- **1 tablespoon vegetable oil**
- **4 ounces bean sprouts**
- **½ tablespoon toasted white sesame seeds, for garnish**
- **½ tablespoon black sesame seeds, for garnish**
- **juice of 1 lemon**
- **Basic Ponzu Sauce**

- Combine carrot, onion, spice sprouts, cucumber and pickled ginger in mixing bowl.

- Heat oil in sauté pan. Stir-fry bean sprouts over high heat for 15 seconds. Transfer to mixing bowl with vegetables and toss.

- Remove tuna from marinade and grill over high heat for 45 seconds to 1 minute per side for medium-rare.

- To serve, divide salad among 4 serving plates. Sprinkle sesame seeds and lemon juice over top. Place tuna on top of salad and spoon Basic Ponzu Sauce over fish.

(Continued)

(Hibachi Tuna with Maui Onion Salad and Ponzu Sauce, continued)

Basic Ponzu Sauce

1 **cup mirin**
¾ **cup light soy sauce**
1 **teaspoon dried red chile flakes, to taste**
2 **tablespoons fresh lemon juice**

- Bring mirin to boil in saucepan and reduce to ⅓ cup (about 5 minutes). Remove from heat and allow to cool. Whisk in soy sauce, chile flakes and lemon juice. Cool to room temperature.

Yields 4 servings, 1¼ cups Ponzu Sauce.

Note: For Sweet Ponzu Sauce, use only ¼ cup of soy sauce and ¼ teaspoon chile flakes. Proportions can be adjusted to taste. Serve with mild-flavored fish.

Ginger Crusted Butterfish with Miso Chili Sauce

Executive Chef Linda Yamada, Nicholas Nickolas Restaurant

1 cup butter, room temperature

1 cup panko

½ chopped ginger

1 teaspoon salt

4 6-ounce filets of frozen butterfish or black cod (defrosted, rinsed, scales removed and patted dry)

Miso Chili Sauce

green onion, julienned

kizami shoga (slivered, seasoned ginger root)

- Preheat oven to broil. Line baking dish with foil.

- In small mixing bowl mix butter, panko, ginger and salt for crust.

- Place butterfish filets in baking dish, without sides touching. Spread crust over top, dividing to cover 4 pieces.

- Broil until brown (about 15 minutes). If crust starts to brown too fast, lower heat to 375° setting. Continue to bake until fish is done.

- On serving plate, spread sauce and then place fish on top. Garnish with green onion and kizami shoga.

Miso Chili Sauce

½ cup red (aka) miso paste

¼ white sugar

¼ rice wine vinegar

¼ water

1 teaspoon sambal (chili paste)

1 tablespoon chopped green onion

1 teaspoon chopped cilantro

- In small mixing bowl stir miso paste and sugar together. Slowly add vinegar and water until smooth, then add remaining ingredients.

Yields 4 servings.

Artichoke Risotto

Chef Mark Adair, Ihilani Resort & Spa

6 cups chicken stock
4 tablespoons unsalted butter, softened
3 cloves shallots, minced
2 cups arborio rice
1 cup dry vermouth
1½ pounds baby artichoke hearts, cooked and halved
1 cup finely grated Parmesan cheese, divided
  kosher salt, to taste
  freshly ground white pepper, to taste

- Warm chicken stock over medium heat and keep warm (130°).

- Melt butter in large saucepan. When butter begins to foam, add shallots and cook until translucent.

- Add rice and cook until coated with butter mixture. Add vermouth and cook until almost fully reduced.

- Add enough stock to barely cover rice. Cook over medium heat, stirring constantly, until stock is almost completely absorbed. Add more stock as it is absorbed. Continue stirring. After 10 minutes cooking, add artichoke hearts and heat through. Rice should be tender, but still firm to the bite. Add ⅓ of cheese and mix in. Texture should be loose and creamy (not gummy and sticky). Add salt and pepper to taste.

- Serve with remaining cheese sprinkled over top.

Yields 6-8 first course servings, 4-6 main course servings.

Glossary & Substitutions

Ahi - Big-eye or yellow fin tuna, a firm, full-flavored tuna enjoyed raw as sashimi.

Aku - Skipjack tuna with deep red firm flesh.

Banana leaves - Used to wrap a variety of island dishes. Substitute parchment paper or aluminum foil.

Bean sprouts (fresh) - These are sprouted mung beans found in the produce section of markets. No substitute provides the same texture or mild taste, particularly when the recipe calls for fresh bean sprouts. Limp canned bean sprouts have a different texture from fresh ones. Substitute these only in cooked dishes.

Char siu - Chinese barbecued pork.

Chili oil - Chiles are steeped in hot (temperature) salad oil.

Chinese 5-Spice - 1 part each ground cinnamon, cloves, fennel seeds, star anise (licorice flavor) and Szechwan peppercorns. Available already mixed in supermarkets and Asian grocery stores.

Chinese parsley - See cilantro.

Chinese noodles - These noodles are either thin and round (chow mein), or wide and flat (chow fun or foon tiu meen), and are made from wheat flour, water and eggs. Substitute American or Italian pasta.

Chinese or chop suey yam - Also known as jicama or yam bean. May substitute water chestnuts.

Cilantro - Also called Chinese parsley. Grown from the coriander spice plant, it has a unique flavor that cannot be substituted. For a green effect, use regular parsley.

Coconut milk - Available frozen or canned, this milk is extracted from the flesh of fresh coconut. Note whether recipe calls for sweetened or unsweetened coconut milk. No substitute available.

Coconut syrup - A mix of coconut water (the liquid found in the center of a coconut), grated fresh coconut, sugar and cream of tartar.

Daikon - A large radish.

Dashi-no-moto - Japanese powdered soup stock.

Dashi konbu - A soup stock from dried seaweed and fish flakes.

Feta cheese - A soft cheese with a sharp and salty flavor, made from ewes' or goats' milk. If used in a filling, substitute well-drained ricotta cheese, but taste the filling carefully for seasoning; if feta is used as a topping, there is no real substitute, so simply use any sharp, salty cheese.

Fish sauce - A Southeast Asia ingredient made by fermenting fish in brine over months in the sun. The sauce keeps indefinitely on the shelf.

Guava - A small yellow or strawberry tropical fruit. Although its flavor is unique, substitute any other tropical fruit.

Haupia - Hawaiian coconut pudding.

Hawaiian chile pepper - Small, spicy, red-orange chile.

Hawaiian salt - Coarse salt, rock salt.

Hoisin sauce (also hoi sin jeong) - A reddish, slightly sweet, pungent, fermented bean sauce seasoned with garlic and chiles. Used as a condiment with dishes such as pork or roast duck and often as an ingredient in marinades. There is no real substitute.

Kaki mochi - Japanese rice crackers.

Kalua - Hawaiian method of cooking foods in an underground pit (imu).

Kinako - Japanese powdered soybean.

Kumu - Goat fish.

Lumpia - Filipino fried spring roll.

Manoa lettuce (Green Mignonette) - Use any soft-leafed, semi-head lettuce such as red-leaf or butter lettuce.

Maui onion - A sweet onion grown on the island of Maui. Use any sweet, round onion such as Vidalia, Texas Sweets, or Walla Walla.

Mirin - Japanese sweet cooking rice wine.

Miso - Fermented soy bean paste used to season soups, sauces and salad dressings.

Mochi - Pounded gluntinous or sweet rice (mochi rice) cakes.

Mochiko - Flour made from glutinous rice.

Nairagi - Striped marlin.

Ogo (limu manauea) - Edible seaweed, sea vegetable or sea sprouts.

Onaga - Long-tailed red snapper.

'Ono - Hawaiian for delicious.

Opakapaka - Pink snapper, a mild, medium-firm fish. Substitute cod, haddock, halibut, tilefish, grouper or tilapia.

Oyster sauce - A thick, salty, rich flavored sauce made from dried oysters.

Panko flakes - A Japanese crispy flour meal for breading. Substitute store-bought bread crumbs but will not have same effect.

Papaya - A tropical fruit with sweet apricot-colored flesh with edible seeds. Substitute mangoes or peaches, but the flavor will be different.

Passion fruit (lilikoi) - It has a tangy, citrus-like taste. A tangy citrus-like taste. The juice is used as a flavoring and sold as a frozen juice concentrate. Substitute mango, guava, peach, or papaya nectar, but the flavor will be different.

Poi - Steamed taro root pounded into a thick paste. It has a bland taste, but takes on the flavor of the food served with it. It was the most important source of starch for Hawaiians.

Poke - Fresh fish cut in cubes and seasoned with seaweed, soy sauce, chili, Hawaiian salt and ginger or inamona (chopped kukui nut). It is usually served as an appetizer.

Ponzu - A sauce based on citrus juice that may be mixed with soy for a dipping sauce. Substitute lemon or lime.

Portuguese sausage - Substitute a spicy Italian sausage (mild or hot) liberally seasoned with red pepper.

Pupu - Finger food. The term is usually associated with snacks or appetizers, but can also refer to relishes.

Rice sticks (rice vermicelli, long rice, cellophane noodles or rice noodles) - These translucent noodles resemble stiff, nylon fishing line. Rice sticks are made from rice flour, while cellophane noodles are made from ground mung beans. Translucent noodles are also called bean threads, yam noodles, silver threads, transparent noodles, bai fun, ning fun, mai fun, fun see, shirataki and harusame. They become slippery and soft when soaked in cool water about 30 minutes. Then they are usually cooked with other ingredients. If dropped into hot oil, they will explode into crisp, white strands for a garnish. (The shirataki will not explode this way, however). Once a soup is hot, substitute regular cooked noodles, but if the recipe calls for dropping the noodles in hot oil, no substitute exists.

Rice vinegar - Japanese vinegar made from rice but less tart and tangy than other vinegars.

Saimin noodles - Substitute any long, thin, round cooked noodles.

Sake - Japanese rice wine. Substitute dry sherry, but the flavor will be different.

Sesame oil - Small quantities of sesame oil are added to other oils or called for in recipes to bring the nutty, concentrated sesame flavor to the dish. No substitute.

Shiitake mushrooms - Substitute an equal amount of any full-flavored, meaty mushroom.

Snow peas (sugar peas, Chinese peas) - Substitute snap peas or any crispy, sweet- or mild-flavored green vegetable such as green beans.

Soba noodles - Japanese noodles made from buckwheat flour.

Somen - Fine Japanese wheat flour noodles.

Ti leaves - Used to wrap a variety of island dishes before cooking. Substitute parchment paper or aluminum foil.

Tofu (dow fu, suey dow fu) - Soy bean curd which has been compressed from the milky liquid from cooked soy beans into a white block. The texture is that of well-baked custard and the blocks are usually packed in water. No substitute exists. Do not substitute bottled Chinese bean cake as it is alcoholic and strong-flavored.

Udon noodles (Japanese wheat noodles) - Substitute any wide, flat, Italian or American noodle.

Wasabi (Japanese green horseradish) - This very hot-tasting, green, horse-radish sauce is green powder and water combined to form a paste. Substitute a mixture of ordinary ground, dry yellow mustard and water blended into the consistency of a paste. Do not substitute regular horseradish.

Won bok (Chinese cabbage, celery cabbage or napa cabbage) - Substitute any pale green cabbage that has a delicate, mild celery-cabbage taste.

Won ton skins/wrappers - Raw pasta rolled into sheets 1/16-inch thick or less and cut into 3-inch squares. They are usually filled with meat, vegetable or seafood mixtures, then folded and fried in oil, steamed or simmered like dumplings in soup. Recipe: Mix and knead 2 cups flour with 3 eggs and 1 teaspoon salt. Sprinkle rolling pin and board with cornstarch; roll 1/4 of the dough into a long, thin rectangle. Let dough rest 10 minutes, then continue rolling until it is about 1/16-inch thick or even thinner. Cut into 3-inch squares. Stack squares with cornstarch between them and wrap in plastic film; proceed with remaining dough. Can be frozen. Makes 6-8 dozen squares.

Contributors

The Child & Family Service Guild thanks with warm *aloha* all of the members and friends of the Guild who contributed recipes, time, talent and support.

Geri Ah Sam
Gerry Alexander
Marilyn Alvine
Susie Anderson
Daisy Asher
JD Aweau
Jackie Aweau
Shea Balika
Connie Baniaga
Tammie Barber
Mary Ann Baybayan
Debbie Bennett
Kit Beuret
Drew Breen
Abby Brown
Mary Jane Brown
Shizuko Bryan
Marie Bunton
Nani Burgo
Chuck Burgo
Dee Dee Carone
Jo-Ann Chang
Suzanne Ching
Jo Ann Chinn
Sandrea Chun
Rita Collet
Patricia Ann Connor
Kathy Croze
Michele D'Amico
Robert P. Daniel
Lyn Fujiyoshi
Gwen Fukuhara
Carla Fukumoto
Elizabeth Fuller
Larry Fuller
Mike Fuller
Suzanne Fuller
Rayna Galati
Joy Ganeku
Jan M. George
Lillian Hamaishi
Mike Han
Linda Harlow
Lori Harrison
Joyce Herbert
Hannelore Herbig
Lance Higa
Amy Hizenski
Kathryn Hunter

Miles Ichida
Marjorie Inn-Francis
Mark Jensen
Jane Jones
Kaylene Kamada
Sharon Karp
Shirlie Katzenberger
Donald Keliinoi
Janice Kelson
Leslie Kissner
Lois Kobayashi
Lester Kodama
Cindy Kodama
Carol Kramer
Barbara Kuljis
Yolanda Kyle
Jonel Lee
Jo Ann Lelepali
Virginia Lippi
Linda Lord
Lawrence Lucero
Nancy Luke
Norma Luke
Barbara Lunow
Lorraine Lunow-Luke
Jill MacMillan
Melinda Manaut
Manu Maunupau
Shirley McCarthy
Krista McCord
Naomi Mihara
Kathy Mills
Miles Miyahara
Thanh Mougeot
Margaret Musser
Nicole Myers
Gayle Nakashima
Sue Norton
Bobbe Nunes
Janelle Ogata
Cathy Ogawa
Polly Oliver
Grace Ono
Marilyn Pappas
Valerie Parsons
Eleanor Pence
Ann V. Perrino
Jennie Phillips

Ginger Plasch
Pam Putnicki
Mildred Ramsey
Anne Rautio
Betty Rhodes
Sandy Rogin
Amy Roper
Moira Schenker
Sandy Segawa
Irene Shibuya
Joanie Shibuya
Nikki Shinsato
Gail Smith
Ginger Smith
Maria Smith
Wanda Sueda
Cheryl Suzuki
Naomi Sutton
Ernestine Tabrah
Muriel Takahashi
Linda Tam
Rhonda Thomas
Patsy Tilton
Bonny Tinebra
Noel Trainor
Suong Tran
June Tsukamoto
Bob Tsushima
Jeanne Tsushima
Kathryn Tsushima
Marian Turney
Jennifer Ulveling
Margi Ulveling
Roger Ulveling
John Utley
Kimi Uto
Lorraine Vinigas
Claire Von Buchwald
Mildred Watanabe
Lynn Watanabe
Mary Ann Whaley
Cindy White
Donna Wiecking
Cynthia Wo
Wallis Yamamoto
Lynda Yonamine
Sandi Yorong
Carolyn Yoshihara

Index

A

Q

R

S

Flavors of Hawaii
Cookbook Order Form

Name _____

Address   City/State/Zip   Phone#

☐ Please send _____ copies of **Flavors of Hawaii**

@ $19.99 each $ _____

Plus shipping and handling @ $4.50 each $ _____

TOTAL AMOUNT $ _____

☐ Please charge $ _____ to my [ ] VISA   [ ] MasterCard

Credit Card No. _____ Exp. Date _____

Name on card _____ Signature _____

Please complete and return to:

Child & Family Service
200 N. Vineyard Blvd., Bldg. B
Honolulu, HI 96817
Tel: (808) 543-8441 Fax: (808) 524-8383

Child&Family
S E R V I C E

Flavors of Hawaii
Cookbook Order Form

Name _____

Address   City/State/Zip   Phone#

☐ Please send _____ copies of **Flavors of Hawaii**

@ $19.99 each $ _____

Plus shipping and handling @ $4.50 each $ _____

TOTAL AMOUNT $ _____

☐ Please charge $ _____ to my [ ] VISA   [ ] MasterCard

Credit Card No. _____ Exp. Date _____

Name on card _____ Signature _____

Please complete and return to:

Child & Family Service
200 N. Vineyard Blvd., Bldg. B
Honolulu, HI 96817
Tel: (808) 543-8441 Fax: (808) 524-8383

Child&Family
S E R V I C E

Flavors of Hawaii
Cookbook Order Form

Name _____

Address _____ City/State/Zip _____ Phone# _____

❑ Please send _____ copies of **Flavors of Hawaii**

@ $19.99 each $ _____

Plus shipping and handling @ $4.50 each $ _____

TOTAL AMOUNT $ _____

❑ Please charge $ _____ to my [ ] VISA   [ ] MasterCard

Credit Card No. _____ Exp. Date _____

Name on card _____ Signature _____

Please complete and return to:

Child & Family Service
200 N. Vineyard Blvd., Bldg. B
Honolulu, HI 96817
Tel: (808) 543-8441 Fax: (808) 524-8383

Flavors of Hawaii
Cookbook Order Form

Name _____

Address _____ City/State/Zip _____ Phone# _____

❑ Please send _____ copies of **Flavors of Hawaii**

@ $19.99 each $ _____

Plus shipping and handling @ $4.50 each $ _____

TOTAL AMOUNT $ _____

❑ Please charge $ _____ to my [ ] VISA   [ ] MasterCard

Credit Card No. _____ Exp. Date _____

Name on card _____ Signature _____

Please complete and return to:

Child & Family Service
200 N. Vineyard Blvd., Bldg. B
Honolulu, HI 96817
Tel: (808) 543-8441 Fax: (808) 524-8383